Teaching Conflict-Related Sexual Violence Through Human Rights Education: The Case of the Japanese Military's "Comfort Women"

I0104824

Jing A. Williams and Phyllis Kim

NCSS

National Council for the Social Studies
8403 Colesville Road • Suite 1100 • Silver Spring, Maryland 20910 • socialstudies.org

NCSS BOARD OF DIRECTORS, 2025–2026
OFFICERS

Tina M. Ellsworth, Ph.D.
PRESIDENT
University of Central Missouri
Warrensburg, MO

David Kendrick
VICE PRESIDENT
Loganville High School
Loganville, GA

Joe Schmidt
PRESIDENT-ELECT
Bill of Rights Institute
Augusta, ME

Jennifer Morgan
PAST PRESIDENT
West Salem Middle School
West Salem, WI

BOARD OF DIRECTORS

Alex Cuenca, Ph.D.
Indiana University
Bloomington, IN (2026)

Heather Nice
The Colonial Williamsburg
Foundation
Williamsburg, VA (2026)

Anne Walker
Edison High School
Alexandria, VA (2028)

Carly Donick
Cabrillo Middle School
Ventura, CA (2026)

Stephanie Nichols
Narragansett Elementary School
Gorham, ME (2028)

Gabriel Valdez
Fort Worth Independent School
District
Fort Worth, TX (2028)

Terrell Fleming
Prince Edward County Public Schools
Farmville, VA (2027)

Renita Parks
Memphis, TN (2028)

EX OFFICIO
Casey Cullen
House of Delegates Steering
Committee Chair (2025–2026)

Kimberly Huffman
Wayne County Schools
Smithville, OH (2024)

Marc Turner
Spring Hill High School
Columbia, SC (2026)

Stephen Masyada
Lou Frey Institute and the Florida
Joint Center for Citizenship
Orlando, FL (2027)

Amy Walker
Olathe Public Schools
Olathe, KS (2027)

NCSS EXECUTIVE DIRECTOR Kelly McFarland Stratman
EDITORIAL STAFF ON THIS PUBLICATION Laura Godfrey, Nancy Driver
DESIGN AND PRODUCTION Rich Palmer

© 2025 National Council for the Social Studies
Silver Spring, MD

Cover image: *Comfort Women Girls*, Acrylic on Korean paper, 210 x 150 cm, 2018, by Kyung-shin Lee.
©2018 by Kyung-shin Lee. Reprinted by permission of the artist.

Library of Congress Control Number: 2025947735

ISBN: 978-0-87986-147-6 (print)
ISBN: 978-0-87986-148-3 (ebook)

*Teaching Conflict-Related Sexual Violence Through Human Rights Education:
The Case of the Japanese Military's "Comfort Women"*

To Grandmas

To educators who refuse to let the history of wartime sexual violence be forgotten

iii

Teaching Conflict-Related Sexual Violence Through Human Rights Education:
The Case of the Japanese Military's "Comfort Women"

Contents

Foreword, by Keith C. Barton v

From the Authors... viii

Acknowledgements ix

Introduction 1

Part I. Learning About Human Rights 5

Chapter 1. The History... 6

Chapter 2. The Denial... 14

Chapter 3. The Responses.. 24

Part II. Learning for Human Rights.. 32

Chapter 4. The Resistance 33

Chapter 5. The Remembrance 39

Afterword, by Audrey Osler... 47

Further Resources on "Comfort Women" Education.. 51

References 55

About the Authors.. 67

Teaching Conflict-Related Sexual Violence Through Human Rights Education:
The Case of the Japanese Military's "Comfort Women"

Foreword

This book provides a useful (and user-friendly) guide to teaching about the Japanese military's "comfort women" as a case of conflict-related sexual violence. At first glance, some educators may see this as a specialized, even marginal topic, but as this work illustrates, the topic brings into focus numerous critical aspects of history and social studies education, each of them relevant to a wide range of settings, contexts, and audiences.

The first of these is the need to help students understand conflict in a more comprehensive way than they usually encounter in the curriculum. Of course, wars (and lower-level conflicts) are a staple of school history, but coverage usually focuses on political, diplomatic, and military aspects of conflict. As important as these are, they can obscure the human impact of war. And although it has become common to include attention to experiences of the ordinary soldier, or in some cases to the impact of war on the "home front," including the impact on women, these too can blunt attention to how wars affect the most vulnerable members of society, particularly those in areas directly affected by conflict (Dang, 2025). It is one thing to acknowledge that food was rationed in warring countries or that soldiers endured difficult, even traumatic circumstances; it is quite another to realize that women during conflict are raped, often repeatedly—even being enslaved as sexual objects, as in the case of "comfort women"—and either die from the experience or bear the trauma for the rest of their lives.

And make no mistake: Although the "comfort women" case is one of the most extreme (and well-documented) examples of conflict-related sexual violence, it is by no means unique. During the U.S. Civil War, Northern troops raped Southern women (and Black women were always subject to rape before, during, and after the war); during World War II, German guards and soldiers raped women in concentration camps and in occupied territories; afterward, U.S. soldiers raped German women during postwar occupation; Korean and U.S. soldiers raped Vietnamese women during the Second Indochina War; warring factions in South Sudan continue to rape women during the ongoing conflict there. Sexual violence is often an explicit strategy of warfare (and even of genocide), but it always occurs whether as a conscious strategy or not. Sexual violence is one of the most significant and pervasive effects of any conflict, and without knowing how women and their bodies are attacked during warfare, students cannot be said to understand war at all. Teaching about warfare without addressing sexual violence is not just misleading or incomplete; it amounts to the erasure of one of the most significant effects of war.

Rape. In classrooms, few educators use this word or other blunt terms such as *sexual violence* or *sexual abuse.* They may be uncertain whether such terms are appropriate for students, and they often assert that their students are not mature enough to encounter these words or to learn about the violent practices that they represent, even at the secondary level. As a result, they often omit sexual violence from the curriculum, or discuss it with vague or euphemistic terms, with the intent of softening the harshness of the subject (Engebretson, 2013). But erasing sexual violence does nothing to help students understand the past (or present), nor does it provide a space for them to work through difficult or traumatic topics so that they better understand the world around them—including, in many cases, their own experiences. And let's face it: Adolescents know what sexual violence is, and they know the word *rape*; a shocking percentage have been victims themselves

(Gewirtz-Meydan & Finkelhor, 2019). We are not protecting them from anything by avoiding these topics, and this is part of the value of including the specific case of "comfort women" forced into sexual slavery: There is no way to discuss it without saying *rape*.

In addition to helping students better understand the impact of conflict, an important outcome of teaching about conflict-related sexual violence is that it can motivate students to care—not only about the victims of a specific instance of violence, but about their own responsibilities to others in the present (Jun, 2020). This book situates the case of "comfort women" within the broader context of human rights education, so that students may draw lessons that extend beyond any one situation. But for human rights to be more than an abstract topic, students must develop an affective commitment to the circumstances of people who may be very different than themselves (Barton & Ho, 2022). Engaging with the voices of survivors of violence can develop precisely that kind of engagement. As Jun (2020) has shown, South Korean students' affective engagement when studying "comfort women" becomes part of their "moral compass" (p. 18), with implications for their ongoing sense of civic responsibility today.

Even when students feel responsible for civic involvement, though, their perspectives can be limited, and this book calls attention to an often-neglected element of education for human rights: the role of institutional practices, such as the work of governments, intergovernmental organizations, and nongovernmental organizations. Even students who have studied human rights and are committed to the topic tend to overemphasize the personal dimension of preventing abuses, such as changing their own attitudes, raising the awareness of others, or donating to charitable causes (Barton, 2020). They have much less familiarity with the kind of institutional pressures that can effectively acknowledge and address human rights issues. In the lessons and resources in this book, students see not only how advocacy organizations have brought the issue of "comfort women" to light but also how present-day efforts to end conflict-related sexual violence depend on tribunals, international sanctions, and diplomatic pressure, all of which are undertaken not by individuals but by national governments and by intergovernmental organizations, such as the United Nations and the European Union. This focus helps students see that protecting human rights is much more than a matter of changing attitudes.

Finally, this book exposes students to another crucial but neglected aspect of history education: the societal context of remembrance, including its often-contested nature. Too often, schools present students with an image of history as something that not only is settled but also is distant from contemporary life. Students have few chances to consider why specific topics in history might have significance outside school or why heated debates occur over what should and should not be remembered. This book devotes extended attention to precisely this issue, as it details the role of memorials, monuments, and days of remembrance and, importantly, the opposition to these by the Japanese government. These lessons give students the chance to see, in very concrete terms, why memorialization holds so much importance in society and what pressures are exerted to prevent some historic events from being remembered. These are perennial issues (and are very much in the news at the time of the publication of this book) and students' understanding of the societal context of history will benefit enormously from these lessons on remembrance and resistance.

In summary, this book—in its background information, its lessons, and its resources—provides educators with a concrete way of addressing crucial but often-overlooked aspects of history and social studies, including conflict-related sexual violence, the institutional practices that protect

vi

Teaching Conflict-Related Sexual Violence Through Human Rights Education:
The Case of the Japanese Military's "Comfort Women"

human rights, and controversies around historical remembrance. Teachers of different subjects, and with different backgrounds and interests, will no doubt adapt these materials to suit their own contexts, but this material provides a strong and meaningful foundation for expanding students' understanding of both past and present.

Keith C. Barton is Professor of Curriculum & Instruction at Indiana University. His work focuses on history education, human rights education, and education for social action in the United States and internationally.

References

Barton, K. C. (2020). Students' understanding of institutional practices: The missing dimension in human rights education. *American Educational Research Journal, 57*(1), 188–217. **https://doi.org/10.3102/0002831219849871**

Barton, K. C., & Ho, L.-C. (2022). *Curriculum for justice and harmony: Deliberation, knowledge, and action in social and civic education.* Routledge.

Dang, Q. (2025, April 23–27). *"It doesn't hurt, but it tickles": Representations of the Vietnam War in the National Archives' teaching resources* [Paper presentation]. American Educational Research Association Annual Meeting, Denver, CO, United States.

Engebretson, K. E. (2013). Grappling with "that awkward sex stuff": Encountering themes of sexual violence in the formal curriculum. *The Journal of Social Studies Research, 37*(4), 195–207. **https://doi.org/10.1016/j.jssr.2013.08.002**

Gewirtz-Meydan, A., & Finkelhor, D. (2019). Sexual abuse and assault in a large national sample of children and adolescents. *Child Maltreatment, 25*(2), 203–214. **https://doi.org/10.1177/1077559519873975**

Jun, H. (2020). "I think the comfort women are us": National identity and affective historical empathy in students' understanding of "comfort women" in South Korea. *The Journal of Social Studies Research, 44*(1), 7–19. **https://doi.org/10.1016/j.jssr.2019.09.005**

vii

Teaching Conflict-Related Sexual Violence Through Human Rights Education: The Case of the Japanese Military's "Comfort Women"

From the Authors

Writing this book has been a deeply challenging and emotional journey for us. The subject matter of conflict-related sexual violence, particularly the harrowing experiences of the Japanese military's "comfort women," is profoundly traumatic. As we delved into these stories, we often found ourselves overwhelmed with sadness and grief. Our grief was heightened when two Grandmas—Won-ok Gil and Ok-seon Lee—passed away while we were working on this book.

To ensure we could continue our work, we had to take regular breaks to process our emotions and regain our strength. These pauses were essential for us to maintain our well-being and to approach the topic with the sensitivity and respect it deserves.

We hope that our readers understand the emotional toll this work has taken on us and appreciate the care and dedication we have put into presenting these important stories and lessons. Our goal is to contribute to human rights education and to honor the memories of those who suffered.

Thank you for joining us on this journey.

viii

Teaching Conflict-Related Sexual Violence Through Human Rights Education:
The Case of the Japanese Military's "Comfort Women"

Acknowledgments

We would like to express our deepest gratitude to our families, whose unwavering support and encouragement sustained us throughout the writing of this book. Your love and patience have been our greatest source of strength.

We are profoundly grateful to Dr. Keith Barton and Dr. Audrey Osler for their invaluable contributions. Dr. Barton's thoughtful foreword sets the stage for the critical discussions that follow, drawing on his vast experience in social studies education to highlight the importance of addressing conflict-related sexual violence through educational frameworks. Dr. Osler's insightful afterword provides a nuanced perspective that deepens the readers' understanding of the complex issues discussed in this book. Her extensive work in human rights education has been a guiding light for us. Her expertise and dedication to social studies and human rights education have been truly inspiring.

Our heartfelt thanks also go to the National Council for the Social Studies (NCSS) for their support in publishing this work. NCSS's commitment to advancing social studies education and promoting human rights awareness has been instrumental in bringing this book to fruition. We are especially grateful to Nancy Driver, former NCSS Director of Publications, whose approval of our book proposal and recognition of its value made this publication possible at a time when many other publishers declined. Her support was pivotal in moving our project forward. We also extend our sincere thanks to Laura Godfrey, whose careful and considerate copyediting significantly enhanced the clarity and quality of our writing. Their contributions, along with NCSS's dedication to fostering critical thinking and informed citizenship, align perfectly with the goals of our manuscript. We are honored to have our work included in their esteemed publications.

Last but not least, we express our profound gratitude to the survivors of conflict-related sexual violence who bravely broke the silence, illuminating the horrors of sexual violence and the lifelong impact of that violence. We are especially inspired by the courage and unwavering dedication of the surviving *Grandmas*—an affectionate term for the victims of Japanese military sexual slavery—who have led the international redress movement since first speaking out in the early 1990s. With so few of them remaining with us, we renew our commitment to raising awareness about this dark chapter in human history and pursuing justice for the victims and their families.

ix

Teaching Conflict-Related Sexual Violence Through Human Rights Education:
The Case of the Japanese Military's "Comfort Women"

Introduction

[Sexual violence] is a way of demonstrating power and control. It inflicts fear on the whole community. And it is unfortunately a very effective, cheap, and silent weapon with a long-lasting effect on every society.

—Margot Wallström,
the United Nations Secretary-General's
Special Representative on Sexual Violence in Conflict

Conflict-related sexual violence (CRSV) has been an ongoing issue in human history. It is as old as war itself. Particularly during the 20th and 21st centuries, CRSV has become an integral part of many wars, "a strategy used intentionally by combatants to harm individuals and to destroy communities" (Rittner et al., 2016, p. 10). Lamb (2020) considers rape in war "the cheapest weapon known to man," noting that

> It devastates families and empties villages. It turns young girls into outcasts who wish their lives over when they are hardly begun. It begets children who are daily reminders to their mothers of their ordeal and are often rejected by their community as "bad blood." And it's almost always ignored in the history books. (p. 3)

As a tactic of war, CRSV has been used by nations to serve various purposes. For example, it can be used as a weapon of genocide (Rittner & Roth, 2012), an organized system to meet the soldiers' sexual needs and humiliate the defeated nations as the Imperial Japanese military did during World War II (Qiu, 2013; Tanaka, 2002; Yoshimi, 1995), a tool for political and economic gains for the host country during and after the Korean War in South Korea (Moon, 1997), a strategy for terror and obedience inflicted upon Ukrainian women by Russian soldiers (Dovhan & Hyun, 2025), or simply as a way to relieve boredom as some American soldiers did in Vietnam (Brownmiller, 1975).

While CRSV was used as a war strategy for genocidal purposes during the conflicts in Bosnia, the former Yugoslavia, and Rwanda, Baaz and Stern (2013) warn readers that not all CRSV is a strategic weapon of war being ordered from above. Based on their research on the conflict in the Democratic Republic of the Congo, they point out that the agency of soldiers, dysfunctional military structures, and the uncertainties of war may also lead to large-scale sexual violence in conflict zones (Baaz & Stern, 2013).

When teaching about war, teachers can easily avoid addressing sexual violence and focus on other aspects of war, such as the political dynamics, propaganda, casualties, leadership, victims, and victories. Then, why teach about CRSV?

When hearing this question, we cannot help but ask, "Why not?" If the purpose of social studies education is "to help young people develop the ability to make informed and reasoned decisions for the public good as citizens of a culturally diverse, democratic society in an interdependent world" (National Council for the Social Studies, 2010, p. 3), teaching about CRSV can well serve that purpose. As Japanese journalist and sexual assault survivor Shiori Ito (2017) said, "rape is a soul-killing experience" (p. 218). CRSV education fosters student compassion toward victims and

1

Teaching Conflict-Related Sexual Violence Through Human Rights Education:
The Case of the Japanese Military's "Comfort Women"

encourages them to become advocates for preventing such atrocities (Williams & Johnson, 2020).

If history teachers avoid discussing CRSV inflicted upon women (and men, in some cases), they are missing out on half the history, which may lead to continued ignorance and future victimization. Iryna Dovhan, a Ukrainian victim of sexual violence in the Russia–Ukraine War, shared in an interview that the silence on CRSV in Ukrainian society contributed to her and other Ukrainian women's suffering:

> I believe this lack of recognition is one of the reasons for the tragic consequences faced by Ukrainian society and women since Russia's full-scale invasion in 2022. Ukrainian society was unaware that Russia was using "conflict-related sexual violence" as a weapon and method of warfare to enforce obedience among the residents of occupied territories. This ignorance allowed many Ukrainian women to openly resist the Russian occupation forces in the early days of the occupation. Many women expressed strong opposition not only to the occupation but also to the presence of Russian troops on Ukrainian soil. As a result, these women were arrested, imprisoned, and subjected to sexual violence by the Russian military. (Dovhan & Hyun, 2025, para. 6)

Silence does not bring peace. Remaining silent on CRSV will not solve the problem; it will only make it worse. What social studies teachers can learn from Dovhan is that they should not and cannot avoid teaching such destructive atrocities, as "they cannot be curbed or prevented unless people are educated about them" (Rittner et al., 2016, p. 23). Denis Mukwege, 2018 recipient of the Nobel Peace Prize, said this in his Nobel lecture: "Turning a blind eye to this tragedy is being complicit. It's not just perpetrators of violence who are responsible for their crimes, it is also those who choose to look the other way" (paras. 35–36).

We write this book because we no longer want this critical topic to be ignored. We have also realized that scarce teaching materials have been published in English to guide social studies teachers in addressing this challenging topic. While we cannot include all CRSV cases in this small book, we highlight one particular case—the Japanese military's "comfort women" system—to show secondary social studies teachers various teaching strategies they can immediately use in their instruction. These same teaching strategies can be applied to other CRSV cases as well.

Why Japanese Military's "Comfort Women"?

The term "comfort women"—*ianfu* in Japanese—is a euphemism coined by the Imperial Japanese Military to refer to the women forced to provide sexual services to Japanese troops at "comfort stations" established by the Japanese military in its occupied territories between 1932 and 1945 (Yoshimi, 1995). The Japanese military's "comfort women" system was the largest scale instance of human trafficking for the sole purpose of providing sex to soldiers in the 20th century, representing a gruesome violation of women's human rights. While it occurred in the Japanese military-occupied areas in East and Southeast Asia before and during World War II, its historical legacy has gone beyond the region and become a global movement (Ruiz, 2020). Artists, filmmakers, nonprofit organizations, human rights activists, scholars, and educators from Asia, North America, Europe, and Australia are working in their respective fields to commemorate this history.

Another reason we highlight the Japanese military's "comfort women" case is due to its

2

Teaching Conflict-Related Sexual Violence Through Human Rights Education:
The Case of the Japanese Military's "Comfort Women"

controversial nature. Despite the ample convincing evidence, Japanese right-wing politicians and their supporters continue to deny the Japanese military's involvement in the "comfort women" system, refuse to acknowledge that these actions constitute war crimes and crimes against humanity, and refuse to accept responsibility (Nishino et al., 2018). To make things worse, revisionists and deniers argue that the "comfort women" history is fictional and attempt to force others to believe in their baseless narratives. A recent example is an article by Ramseyer (2021), a Harvard law professor, who falsely claimed that all Korean "comfort women" were well-paid, voluntary prostitutes who knowingly and willingly entered legal contracts. This article ignited a worldwide uproar over "comfort women" denials (Binkley, 2021; Dudden, 2021; Gerson, 2021), denials that come from within the Japanese government as well. If this history is covered in history textbooks in other countries, Japanese politicians would pressure the publisher to remove the content (McCurry, 2015). When a "comfort woman" statue is erected in a foreign land, Japanese officials often pressure local authorities to remove it (M. Kim, 2024). In 2018, after the City of San Francisco officially accepted the "comfort women" memorial as a city asset, Osaka (a Japanese city) severed its 60-year sister city relationship with San Francisco in protest (McCurry, 2018). Thus, the "comfort women" issue serves as a crucial case for students to engage with and refine their critical thinking skills.

This history needs to be taught in secondary schools in the United States for three reasons: enhancing global awareness, creating human rights awareness, and promoting humanistic teaching (Williams & Johnson, 2020).

First, teaching about the history of the Japanese military's "comfort women" system enhances American students' global awareness of World War II. Numerous studies have found that American students lack knowledge of the Asia–Pacific Theater of World War II (Gruhl, 2010; Olwell, 2011; Williams & Pirlet, 2021). In the early 1930s, Imperial Japan had already begun invading other Asian countries through events such as the Mukden Incident on September 18, 1931. Japan's aggression in Asia occurred years before Hitler invaded Poland in 1939. Learning about the conflicts in the Asia–Pacific Theater will help our students better understand the postwar development of our world, particularly the U.S. government's geopolitical interest in that region.

Second, the Japanese military's "comfort women" system is a typical case study of difficult history and fits into the human rights education framework. Although the Universal Declaration of Human Rights was created after World War II, the Imperial Japanese Army violated many international laws at the time on the "comfort women" issue, including the 1907 Hague Convention IV and annexed regulation, the 1921 International Convention for the Suppression of the Traffic in Women and Children, the 1926 Slavery Convention, the 1929 Geneva Convention, the 1930 Convention Concerning Forced Labour, the Trafficking Conventions of 1904, 1910, and 1933, and the Customary International Humanitarian Law (Argibay, 2003). "Comfort women" were deprived of freedom, which is central to their human rights, and forced sex is a form of slavery and torture.

Third, teaching the history of the Japanese military's "comfort women" system reflects humanistic teaching. Wars are not only about dates, places, names, or statistics. If teachers genuinely want to show their students the destructive nature of war, they have to teach regular people's suffering during war. Teaching is a humanistic activity and should be for the common good (Barton & Levstik, 2004). History education should never be condensed to a prescribed checklist based on content standards alone. The lack of humanism in teaching "has resulted in lack of conscience and caring

Teaching Conflict-Related Sexual Violence Through Human Rights Education:
The Case of the Japanese Military's "Comfort Women"

throughout the ages and throughout the globe," which has led to "human suffering, oppression, fanaticism, and wholesale slaughter of human life under a political or religious ideology that mocks the individual and is suffused with hatred, brute force, and terrorism" (Ornstein, 2015, p. 78). As more people learn about the issue, we can hope that the Japanese right-wing government will eventually be pressured to admit its wrongdoings in history and give victims their belated justice.

Framework of the Book

While there are different approaches to teaching CRSV, this book shows educators how to teach such topics through human rights education, which refers to "all learning that develops the knowledge, skills, and values of human rights" (Flowers, 2000, p. 7). According to the United Nations Declaration on Human Rights Education and Training, human rights education encompasses three dimensions:

(a) Education about human rights, which includes providing knowledge and understanding of human rights norms and principles, the values that underpin them and the mechanisms for their protection;

(b) Education through human rights, which includes learning and teaching in a way that respects the rights of both educators and learners;

(c) Education for human rights, which includes empowering persons to enjoy and exercise their rights and to respect and uphold the rights of others. (United Nations, 2011, Article 2)

Though it is outside the scope of this book, the second dimension—education through human rights—is something that we hope teachers can foster during teaching. Therefore, readers will find this teaching guide is structured based on the other two dimensions: learning about human rights and learning for human rights, which are considered the "two essential objectives" of human rights education (Flowers, 2000, p. 20).

Structure of the Book

This book consists of two parts. The first part—Learning About Human Rights—comprises three chapters covering the history, denial, and international communities' responses to CRSV. The second part—Learning for Human Rights—contains two chapters on the resistance and remembrance of CRSV.

At the beginning of each chapter, we present readers with various CRSV cases from around the world to illustrate the chapter's theme. Next, we highlight the Japanese military's "comfort women" case, followed by a 45-minute, ready-to-use lesson plan, which features teaching strategies teachers can apply to other CRSV cases.

As we planned the lessons, we decided not to use graphic texts, images, or videos. Our decision was made from two considerations. First, we aim to avoid subjecting students to emotional distress or potential trauma, which could hinder their ability to engage with the material or lead them to seek counseling. Such outcomes would not support their learning or well-being. Second, the ultimate goal of CRSV education is to help young students connect to the human rights issue, and any CRSV case teachers introduce in class serves as a steppingstone to a deeper understanding of human rights. We argue that teachers can achieve this ultimate goal without using graphic content.

4

Teaching Conflict-Related Sexual Violence Through Human Rights Education:
The Case of the Japanese Military's "Comfort Women"

Part I. Learning *About* Human Rights

In war, there is no victory for women, no matter which side wins. Women are the worst victims of war and hence the highest stakeholders for peace.

—Noeleen Heyzer,
UNIFEM, now UN Women
(as cited in Barstow, 2000, p. 1)

Human rights education begins with the knowledge of human rights. The Universal Declaration of Human Rights (UDHR) (United Nations [UN], 1948) summarizes the fundamental human rights in its 30 articles, which cover (a) fundamental principles (Article 1 & Article 2); (b) rights of the individual (Article 3–Article 11); (c) rights of the individual in civic and political society (Article 12–Article 17); (d) spiritual, public, and political freedoms (Article 18–Article 21); (e) social, economic, and cultural rights (Article 22–Article 27); and (f) final principles to tie the previous articles together (Article 28–Article 30). Human rights education is cosmopolitan as it usually goes beyond a nation's border and includes all human beings across the globe (Osler, 2016). All students have the right to know what their human rights entail so they can learn how to protect these rights of themselves and others (Barton, 2019).

The UDHR is beyond a declaration. It is a philosophical principle for moral world order, the basis of our knowledge and discussions on human rights, the foundation of international laws, and the ethical standards a government should establish to protect its citizens (Landorf, 2009). As human rights education is gaining momentum in the school curriculum, the UDHR should also become a key document for students to learn about their inalienable rights and for teachers to base the design of their lesson plans.

In Part I, teachers will read about the history, denial, and responses from the international community toward conflict-related sexual violence (CRSV) and the ways CRSV breaches the moral principles of UDHR.

5

Teaching Conflict-Related Sexual Violence Through Human Rights Education:
The Case of the Japanese Military's "Comfort Women"

Chapter 1. The History

It has probably become more dangerous to be a woman than a soldier in an armed conflict.

—Major General Patrick Cammaert,
United Nations Division Commander for
Eastern Democratic Republic of the Congo

Conflict-Related Sexual Violence Worldwide Since the 20th Century

Although the history of conflict-related sexual violence (CRSV) is as old as war itself, it has been largely ignored until the past two decades. To provide a focused overview, we will begin with significant instances of CRSV from the 20th century onward, a period that, though relatively recent, marks a critical point in the history of sexual violence in conflicts. One of the earliest examples of this violent pattern occurred in August 1914, when the German invasion of Belgium led to widespread sexual violence against Belgian women. This pattern was tragically repeated when German forces advanced into France in September (Brownmiller, 1975).

In 1929, the International Committee of the Red Cross adopted the Geneva Convention Relative to the Treatment of Prisoners of War, recognizing that "women shall be treated with all consideration due to their sex" (Article 3). However, Japan and Germany violated this principle within just a few years.

In World War II, both Japan and Germany used rape and sexual violence as tools to achieve their ultimate goal, that is, the humiliation and destruction of "inferior peoples" and the establishment of their absolute control and terror (Brownmiller, 1975, p. 49). In the Asia–Pacific Theater, the Japanese Imperial Armed Forces inflicted sexual violence against women and girls in occupied areas by setting up a sexual slavery system known as "comfort stations," which were military brothels established to meet the soldiers' sexual needs. The earliest "comfort stations" were set up in Shanghai, China, in 1932 (Yoshimi, 1995). Hundreds of thousands of young women and girls from Korea, China, Taiwan, Japan, the Philippines, and other Southeast Asian countries were subjected to this form of sexual violence (Yoshimi, 1995). In Europe, the Nazi German Army sexually assaulted women in the occupied areas, such as Poland, the Netherlands, Estonia, Latvia, and Lithuania. During the Holocaust, sexual violence against Jewish women was also prevalent (Fangrad, 2013; Hedgepeth & Saidel, 2010). In the final months of the war, when the Soviet Red Army and the Western Allies advanced into Germany, sexual violence was widely committed against German women throughout Germany (Anonymous, 2005; Gebhardt, 2015/2017; Grossmann, 1995; Hall, 2010; Köpp, 2010; Lawlor, 2022; Sander, 1992; Stone, 2024; Teo, 1996).

During the Korean War (1950–1953), the South Korean government adopted the Japanese military's "comfort women" system, recruiting Korean women to serve its soldiers (G. Kim, 2011; Moon, 1997). After the armistice was signed, these women began serving American soldiers in the South Korean military camptowns known as *kijichon*, meaning the "commercial districts of small villages that are solely dependent on a U.S. military customer base (Lee, 2018, p. 771). The South Korean government considered *kijichon* women "dollar-earning patriots" (Choe, 2023) and

6

Teaching Conflict-Related Sexual Violence Through Human Rights Education:
The Case of the Japanese Military's "Comfort Women"

"personal ambassadors" (Moon, 1997, p. 153). In the 1960s, camptowns contributed 25% of South Korea's gross national product (Moon, 1997, p. 44). The camptown history is a history of human trafficking, sexual exploitation, and human rights violations against women (Williams, 2025).

Rape and sexual violence against women were rampant and widespread during the Vietnam War (1955–1975). Thousands of Vietnamese women were subjected to rape and other forms of sexual assault by U.S. and South Korean soldiers. The most infamous case was the My Lai massacre on March 16, 1968. During this tragic event, U.S. Army soldiers raped, mutilated, and murdered women and children as young as 12 years old (Rittner & Roth, 2012). The exact number of victimized women and children is unknown.

Entering the 1990s, the world continued witnessing sexual violence in war zones. UN Women (n.d.) provides statistics showing the horrendous reality of women's situation in war zones:

> The data available reflect alarming levels of rape during conflict and its aftermath: Between 250,000 and 500,000 women and girls were raped in the 1994 genocide in Rwanda, more than 60,000 in the civil war in Sierra Leone, between 20,000 and 50,000 in the war in Bosnia and Herzegovina and at least 200,000 in the Democratic Republic of the Congo since 1996. Though shocking, in most cases these data are serious underestimates of the actual numbers of victims, most of whom never report to authorities. (para. 2)

These big numbers may not resonate with most people because our brains are wired to deal with smaller, more tangible numbers that we can easily visualize or relate to everyday experiences. Let's put these numbers into perspective. Imagine an airplane with 200 passengers on board crashes with no survivors. The shock would be immense. Now, imagine this tragedy occurring every single day for 3 to 7 years. That is the scale of sexual violence faced by women and girls during the 1994 Rwandan genocide. Estimates range from 250,000 to 500,000 victims, an incredibly wide span that reflects the difficulty of documenting atrocities of this magnitude. These figures, while staggering, likely underrepresent the true scale of suffering, as many cases remain unreported or undocumented.

After the war in Darfur broke out in 2003, sexual violence against women was used as a weapon to humiliate, punish, terrorize, and displace women and their communities. As an Amnesty International (2011) report stated,

> Violence against women is occurring in a context of systematic human rights violations against civilians in Darfur. The grave violations of international human rights and humanitarian law committed by the Janjawid and the Sudanese army against civilians have targeted men, women and children indiscriminately. Women have been summarily or indiscriminately killed, bombed, raped, tortured, abducted and forcibly displaced. Children have been summarily or indiscriminately killed, tortured, abducted and forcibly displaced; girls have, like women, been the particular target of rapes, abductions and sexual slavery. (Pt. 3, "Violence Against Women in Darfur," para. 2)

During the Yazidi genocide (2014–2017), the Islamic State of Iraq and Syria (ISIS) committed genocidal rape against thousands of Yazidi women and girls, who were abducted and sold into

7

Teaching Conflict-Related Sexual Violence Through Human Rights Education:
The Case of the Japanese Military's "Comfort Women"

slavery and subjected to systematic sexual and psychological abuse (Human Rights Watch, 2016; Murad, 2017). Nadia Murad (2018), a survivor of ISIS sexual slavery and one of the two 2018 Nobel Peace Prize recipients, is fighting to end the exploitation of women and children and hold criminals accountable.

After Russia's full-scale invasion of Ukraine, systematic sexual violence has been inflicted upon Ukrainian girls and women from 15 to 83 years of age (Human Rights Council, 2024). The war is brutal for Ukrainian male soldiers, but it is even more challenging for female soldiers as they usually face cruel torture and rape if captured (Janoski, 2025).

According to the report of the United Nations (UN) Secretary-General (2024), from January to December 2023, sexual violence in conflict settings occurred in the following countries: Afghanistan, the Central African Republic, Colombia, the Democratic Republic of the Congo, Iraq, Israel, the State of Palestine, Libya, Mali, Myanmar, Somalia, South Sudan, Sudan, Syrian Arab Republic, Ukraine, and Yemen.

In June 2025, the Dinah Project released its newest report on the situation of victims and survivors of sexual violence during the Hamas attack on October 7, 2023, and beyond. Some key findings in the report include (a) "sexual violence was widespread and systematic during the October 7 attack," (b) "clear patterns emerged in how the sexual violence was perpetrated," (c) "sexual violence continued in captivity," and (d) "most victims were permanently silenced" (pp. 14–15).

In the next section, we use the Japanese military's "comfort women" system as a case study, providing teachers with historical details, accompanied by a 45-minute lesson plan about the history of "comfort women" through the lens of human rights.

History of Japanese Military's "Comfort Women"

In the mid-19th century, influenced by Western imperialism, Emperor Meiji (1852–1912) started a series of political, social, educational, and cultural reforms in Japan. Following the Meiji Restoration (1868–1889) and the continual modernization process, Japan had become an imperial nation by the end of the 19th century. Japan colonized Taiwan in 1895 and annexed Korea in 1910 as part of Japan's imperial expansion. In the early 1930s, the Imperial Japanese Army invaded Manchuria and established a puppet government in northeast China, positioning itself for further conquest. A full-scale war between China and Japan broke out outside Beijing in the summer of 1937.

After securing victories in the Beijing–Tianjin region, the Japanese army quickly moved south to Shanghai, where it faced fierce resistance. Chiang Kai-shek, the leader of the Nationalist Party, deployed his best troops to defend the city. Despite their efforts, the Japanese forces emerged victorious after three months of intense fighting in the Battle of Shanghai. The Japanese forces, exhausted and unprepared for the harsh winter, continued their advance toward Nanjing, the former capital of China. Along the way, widespread atrocities, including mass rape of women, were reported (Akira, 2008). Upon entering Nanjing on December 13, 1937, the Japanese soldiers unleashed horrific acts of violence, later known as the Nanjing Massacre or the Rape of Nanjing. During the next six weeks, approximately 300,000 Chinese civilians were killed, and an estimated 20,000–80,000 girls and women were raped (Chang, 1997, p. 89).

The international media condemned the brutal sexual violence perpetrated by the Japanese Imperial Army in Nanjing. To regulate its soldiers' behavior and restore Japan's reputation, the

8

Teaching Conflict-Related Sexual Violence Through Human Rights Education:
The Case of the Japanese Military's "Comfort Women"

Japanese military expanded the "comfort station" system (i.e., military brothels) as a general policy across the Indo-Pacific region in late 1937 (Tanaka, 2002). This system was purportedly designed to meet soldiers' sexual demands while preventing further sexual violence and limiting the spread of venereal diseases among soldiers (Yoshimi, 1995). However, in practice, the "comfort station" system failed to achieve either objective (Gruhl, 2010; Tanaka, 2002; Yoshimi, 1995). Figure 1.1 shows places where the Japanese military established and maintained "comfort stations" based on Japanese military records, survivors' testimonies, and Japanese soldiers' memoirs.

Figure 1.1 *Map of "Comfort Stations" of the Japanese Military*

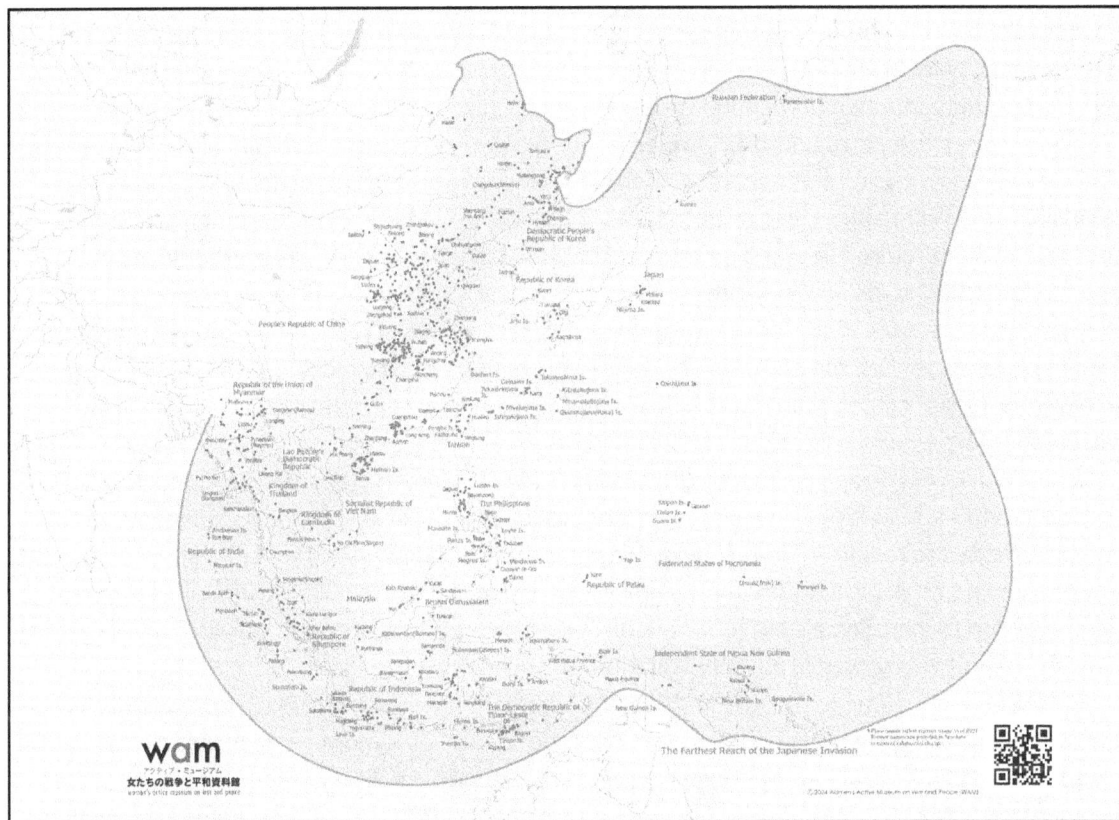

Note. Copyright Women's Active Museum on War and Peace (WAM, n.d.-a; **https://wam-peace.org/ianjo**). Reprinted with permission. See **https://wam-peace.org/download/map-dl-en.html** for a full size, high-resolution map.

The Japanese military forcibly mobilized hundreds of thousands of women and girls from China, Indonesia, Japan, Korea, the Philippines, Taiwan, and other parts of Southeast Asia and the Pacific islands. Initially, recruitment began in Japan proper, primarily from the existing government-sanctioned prostitution system (Hicks, 1994; Norma, 2016; Tanaka, 2002). However, as Japan's warfront expanded into China and Southeast Asia, the military increasingly relied on private recruiters to procure young and inexperienced girls, particularly from its colony, Korea, where Japanese law prohibiting child prostitution was not enforced (Yoshimi, 1995). Many underage girls were deceptively or forcibly taken, with false promises of lucrative jobs abroad, and some girls were sold by destitute families to pay off debts (Choi & Yang, 2023; Qiu, 2013; Schellstede, 2000;

Yoshimi, 1995, 2018). While a small number of women voluntarily entered the system, knowing the nature of the work, the vast majority were recruited through deception, coercion, or outright abduction (Nishino, 2018; Yoshimi, 1995, 2018).

Japanese military and police authorities facilitated the transportation of these women on military vehicles, trains, and ships, allowing them to cross borders with special permits. As Kim-Gibson (1999) noted, "They were nothing more than the military supplies of the Emperor" (p. 40), and their deaths were not recorded. In Japanese military-occupied territories, women—many of whom were teenagers as young as 11—were often seized from their homes, fields, or the streets at gunpoint (Oh, 2001; Qiu, 2013; Tanaka, 2002; Yoshimi, 1995).

Once taken to the "comfort stations," the women lost all freedom and were subjected to sexual slavery. Many were brutally raped daily, with some enduring up to 40 assaults per day (NBC News, 2014). They were stripped of their identities, assigned Japanese names, and forbidden from speaking their native languages (Ruff-O'Herne, 2008). Medical treatment for illnesses, apart from venereal diseases, was rare. Pregnant women were forced to undergo abortions, and those who gave birth saw their babies killed or taken away (Hicks, 1994). Many of these women attempted suicide, and numerous others died by suicide. Those who tried to escape were either killed or severely punished as a warning to others. Escape was nearly impossible in foreign lands where they had no knowledge of the language nor means to return home (Yoshimi, 1995). As Japan faced imminent defeat toward the end of World War II, the military destroyed large amounts of records to cover up its war crimes. Many "comfort women" were massacred before the Japanese army retreated (Morris-Suzuki, 2015).

During World War II, approximately 90% of the "comfort women" perished (Blakemore, 2025). For the survivors, returning home was often not an option. Fear of shame and social ostracization compelled many to remain in foreign lands (Yoshimi, 1995). Those who did return suffered lifelong physical and psychological trauma. Many never married or started families due to infertility or a deep aversion to men. Some survivors were disowned by their families upon learning about their past. As a result, many lived in poverty, isolation, and ill health (H. Kim, 2012).

In 1991, Hak-sun Kim became the first "comfort woman" survivor from South Korea to break the silence and tell the world about her wartime experience. Soon, more survivors began to stand up and voice their horrendous past experiences as the Japanese military's "comfort women." They demanded legal reparations and the Japanese government's official acknowledgment and apology. However, over 80 years after the end of World War II, they have not received either. The several surviving "comfort women" are still fighting the Japanese government for justice.

10

Teaching Conflict-Related Sexual Violence Through Human Rights Education:
The Case of the Japanese Military's "Comfort Women"

Lesson Plan: *How Was the "Comfort Women" System a Human Rights Violation?*

Description
This lesson teaches the history of "comfort women" through a human rights lens. Featured teaching strategies include a video analysis, small group discussions, and a five-minute journaling exercise.

Objectives
By the end of this lesson, students will be able to
- describe the historical background of the "comfort women" issue, and
- articulate how the "comfort women" system is a violation of women's human rights.

NCSS Theme
❷ TIME, CONTINUITY, AND CHANGE

Sources
- Source A: Universal Declaration of Human Rights (UDHR), Articles 1–5 (**www.un.org/en/about-us/universal-declaration-of-human-rights**)
- Source B: *My Sisters in the Stars—The Story of Lee Yong-soo* [Video], by I. Kim, August 4, 2024 (**www.youtube.com/watch?v=GkPclUSl1ml**)

Lesson Activities (45 minutes)
Opening Discussion (5 minutes)
Before introducing the topic of "comfort women," ask students, *Have you heard of human rights? What do human rights mean to you?* Then, have students read Articles 1–5 of UDHR (Source A) and ask, *What does each article mean to you?* Let students share their thoughts freely.

Mini-Lesson: History of "Comfort Women" (10 minutes)
Tell students that they are going to learn about the history of "comfort women," a case that shows how women's human rights have been violated during wartime. Teachers can use the content of this chapter as a starting point to create a mini-lecture on the history of "comfort women." For more content of the "comfort women" history, teachers can visit the following online resources:
- Comfort Women Resource Center, UCLA Center for Korean Studies (**https://www.international.ucla.edu/cks/care/introduction/245347**)
- Fact Sheet on Japanese Military "Comfort Women," *Asia-Pacific Journal: Japan Focus* (**https://apjjf.org/asia-pacific-journal-feature/4829/article**)
- "Teaching about the Comfort Women during World War II and the Use of Personal Stories of the Victims" by B. M. Lee Bisland, J. Kim, and S. Shin, 2019, *Education About Asia*, 24(3) (**www.asianstudies.org/publications/eaa/archives/teaching-about-the-comfort-women-during-world-war-ii-and-the-use-of-personal-stories-of-the-victims**)

The purpose of this short lecture is to provide students with just enough background knowledge of "comfort women" so they can use the information to complete the next activity.

Video Analysis (15 minutes)
Show the short video *My Sisters in the Stars* by Ian Kim (Source B), a high school student who made this video during the 2022–2023 academic year. This animation is based on Grandma Yong-soo Lee's experience as a former "comfort woman."
   After watching the video, ask students the following questions and host a class discussion:
   - What was Grandma Lee's life like when she was young?
   - How old was Grandma Lee when she became a "comfort woman"?
   - Did she willingly become a "comfort woman"? How did she become a victim?
   - Where was Grandma Lee confined as a "comfort woman"?
   - How was she treated at the "comfort station"?
   - How old was she when she was able to go back to Korea?
   - Was she welcomed by her mother? Why?
   - How did her wartime experience impact her later life?

Small Group Discussions (10 minutes)
Put students into small groups of three or four. Instruct them to reread the first five articles of UDHR and discuss one question: *How was the "comfort women" system a human rights violation?* As students discuss within their groups, the teacher should walk around, listen, and observe the discussions. When group discussion is finished, allow each group to share their answers with the rest of the class.

Five-Minute Journaling (5 minutes)
Instruct students to take out a notebook and start a five-minute journal. Start the journal entry with the following sentence: *Today in class, I learned about the history of "comfort women."*

Assessments
   1. Small Group Discussions: This activity allows students to explain how the human rights of "comfort women" were violated.
   2. Five-Minute Journaling: Students' reflection will demonstrate their understanding of the "comfort women" history.

Accommodations
   - If a student has a hearing impairment, the teacher can print out the transcript of the video and give the student a copy before class.
   - If a student is an English language learner, the teacher can use AI to translate the video transcript and give the student both English and translated versions of the transcript.
   - If a student has a vision impairment, the teacher can print out the slides before class and give them to the student during the lecture.

12

Teaching Conflict-Related Sexual Violence Through Human Rights Education:
The Case of the Japanese Military's "Comfort Women"

Extension Activities

Teachers can use other "comfort women" stories in the lesson, followed by a class discussion. The Comfort Women Resource Center includes various testimonies on the "Comfort Women" Speak Up webpage (**www.international.ucla.edu/cks/care/comfortwomen_speakup**).

13

Teaching Conflict-Related Sexual Violence Through Human Rights Education:
The Case of the Japanese Military's "Comfort Women"

Chapter 2. The Denial

The "perfect crime" does not consist in killing the victim or the witness … but rather in obtaining the silence of the witness, the deafness of the judges, and the inconsistency (insanity) of the testimony.

—Jean-François Lyotard,
The Differend: Phrases in Dispute

Denials of Conflict-Related Sexual Violence Worldwide

Throughout history, most aggressor nations have rarely admitted to committing rape (Brownmiller, 1975). Their denials can take on many different forms that can sometimes be mixed with one another. Psychologist and genocide scholar Israel W. Charny asserted that denial was "intrinsically a hate speech" and "a poison which pollut[ed] the human spirit of victims and everybody who [became] associated with it" (AGBU Video, 2021, 0:09, 2:22). Charny (2003) further asserted,

> Denials are celebrations of destruction, renewed humiliations of survivors and all others who care about the destruction of life, attacks on the identity of the victim people, unabashed attempts to dominate the minds of people by dictatorial fiat, and metaphorically, "murders" of historical truth and collective memory. (p. 11)

Although Charny's scholarship primarily focused on genocides, his analysis of denials on genocide applies to conflict-related sexual violence (CRSV). In his classification of denials of the Holocaust and other genocides, Charny (2003) provides an enlightening, heuristic framework for scholars to understand the different forms of denials. He categorized the denials into six groups.

The first group is the malevolent bigotry, which includes two types of denials: denials by perpetrators and denials by those who, while not directly involved, uphold the tradition of bigotry. Soon after the Russia–Ukraine conflict escalated to a full-scale war in 2022, the Russian military was accused of committing sexual violence against Ukrainian girls and women. However, the Kremlin's press service rejected these allegations. Moscow justified its actions as a special military operation in Ukraine and denied committing war crimes (Plucinska et al., 2022). Another case occurred during the Vietnam War when Vietnamese women were subjected to sexual violence by American and South Korean soldiers. However, neither the U.S. government nor the South Korean government have offered official apologies (Barsocchini, 2017; Griffin, 2019).

The second group is self-serving opportunism, referring to denials "in the service of personal or collective self-interest or power such as careerism, pragmatism, exhibitionism and realpolitik" (Charny, 2003, p. 16). These deniers are usually nonperpetrators who may not be bigots, but their influence can be just as detrimental. The most typical case is some scholars in academia who deny the Holocaust or the existence of the Japanese military "comfort women" for "personal gain, economic advantage, or even more simply career advantage" (Charny, 2001, p. 4).

The third group is "innocent denials," based on an extreme interpretation of free speech that defends the unqualified right of deniers to present their views. These deniers "feel good in undertaking seeming 'open-mindedness' of listening to the 'other side' of the argument" (Charny, 2001, p. 5). Examples can be found in the academic debate over the Japanese military "comfort women" issue. For instance, Ward and Lay (2019) presented the Korean perspective advocating justice for "comfort women" and the denialist viewpoint opposing such justice, making their work highly controversial.

The fourth group is "'definitionalism' or insistence on defining cases of mass murders as *not genocide*" (Charny, 2003, p. 22). This approach can also manifest in the denial or minimization of CRSV as a component of genocide, such as the systematic use of rape during the Armenian genocide. However, the Turkish government has repeatedly denied that there was a genocide of the Armenian people (Bedrossian, 2021). In 2021, when U.S. President Joe Biden officially acknowledged the Armenian Genocide, Turkish President Recep Erdogan condemned the statement and criticized the United States for taking what he called "the wrong step" (CBS News, 2021, 0:14).

The fifth group is nationalistic pride, in which denials stem from indifference to the suffering of other victims. At the end of World War II, the Soviet Red Army committed mass rapes against German women. Soviet leadership and propaganda justified these actions as retribution against the Nazis, disregarding the suffering of German civilians, including women. The Soviet government denied these crimes for decades, portraying the Red Army as liberators rather than perpetrators of atrocities (Westervelt, 2009).

The last group is human shallowness, "the dulling and depletion of a genuine sense of tragedy and moral outrage" (Charny, 2003, p. 32). This last form of denial is frequently observed in discussions of CRSV. Sexual violence has often been dismissed as an inevitable byproduct of war (Brownmiller, 1975) or as "war's dirty secret" (Barstow, 2000). The assumption that rape is unavoidable in conflict is widespread. When sexual violence occurs in conflict in remote areas of Africa or the Middle East, where is the world's outrage? What if the victims were from your family, your school, or your hometown? What if they were people you knew, lived near, or shared a community with? These questions challenge the moral detachment that Charny (2003) describes, urging us to confront the human cost of denial and reclaim a sense of collective outrage and empathy.

In the next section, we examine the denial of the Japanese military's "comfort women." The Japanese government, along with certain scholars aligned with its stance, has actively denied and sought to rewrite the "comfort women" history. What have they done to whitewash this war crime? What can we learn from their denial? The next section provides teachers with essential information about the denial of the "comfort women" history, followed by a 45-minute lesson plan. Using primary source documents, the lesson first shows students how the Japanese government denies the "comfort women" issue, and then, students are engaged in inquiry-based learning by analyzing survivors' testimonies to counter-argue the Japanese government's stance on this issue. Featured teaching strategies include small group work and discussions, whole class discussions, document analysis, and political cartoon analysis.

The Denial of "Comfort Women"

The first public testimony of Hak-sun Kim in 1991 encouraged other survivors to come forward, leading to a wave of similar accounts from "comfort women" survivors in Korea and other countries. Throughout the 1990s, multiple lawsuits were filed by survivors from various countries against the

Japanese government, demanding an official apology and compensation. Around the same time, Japanese historian Yoshiaki Yoshimi unearthed and exposed military documents that provided clear evidence of the Imperial Japanese military's direct involvement in establishing and operating the "comfort station" system. As survivors brought their testimonies to the United States and the United Nations (UN), international awareness of Japan's military sexual slavery grew.

Japan's Initial Responses

In 1993, then-Chief Cabinet Secretary Yohei Kono (equivalent to the U.S. Secretary of State) issued a landmark statement known as the Kono Statement (Ministry of Foreign Affairs of Japan, 1993). In the statement, he acknowledged the Japanese military's involvement in the establishment and management of "comfort stations," the coercive and deceptive nature of the recruitment process, and the inhumane conditions that caused immense suffering for the women. The statement promised to "face squarely the historical facts as described above instead of evading them" and "never to repeat the same mistake by forever engraving such issues in our memories through study and teaching of history" (Ministry of Foreign Affairs of Japan, 1993, para. 6).

In 1995, the Japanese government established the "Asian Women's Fund" to raise money from the Japanese public to provide the so-called "atonement money" for surviving "comfort women" in the form of medical and welfare support (Ministry of Foreign Affairs of Japan, 1995). However, this initiative sparked significant controversy in Japan and internationally, as it was perceived as an attempt to provide hush money rather than legal compensation. Critics argued that because the fund was from private donations and did not include an official apology or acknowledgment of Japan's use of military sexual slavery, it circumvented formal governmental responsibility (Onishi, 2007). While some victims accepted the money due to poverty and lack of alternative support, the majority rejected it, considering the initiative an added insult (Comfort Women Resource Center, n.d.). The Japanese government's official stance on the issue continues to downplay the nature and scale of military sexual slavery (Ministry of Foreign Affairs of Japan, n.d.).

Japan's Historical Revisionism on the "Comfort Women" Issue

Under the leadership of former Prime Minister Shinzo Abe, Japan's highly conservative government actively engaged in historical revisionism, seeking to erase, revise, and whitewash its war crimes and the history of the "comfort women" system on the international stage. In March 2007, Abe made international headlines by denying that the "comfort women" were coerced (NBC News, 2007). His statement contributed to the unanimous passage of House Resolution 121 (2007) by the U.S. House of Representatives (see Chapter 3 for more information), which urged Japan to formally accept responsibility for its system of institutionalized sexual slavery during the Pacific War. Japan's historical revisionist efforts have included attempts to dismantle memorials, remove references to the issue from U.S. history textbooks, and apply political obstructions at the UN and the United Nations Educational, Scientific and Cultural Organization (UNESCO).

Dismantling Memorials

After the first *Statue of Peace* (commonly known as the *Girl Statue*, depicting a seated girl with an empty chair beside her; see Figure 5.1) was erected in Glendale, California, in 2013, Japan's conservative newspaper *Sankei Shimbun* coined the term "History War" to urge Japan's response

Teaching Conflict-Related Sexual Violence Through Human Rights Education:
The Case of the Japanese Military's "Comfort Women"

against the growing international awareness and activism surrounding the issue (Yamaguchi, 2020). Shortly thereafter, two Japanese American residents of California filed a lawsuit against the City of Glendale, seeking to remove the statue. The case was ultimately dismissed, with rulings against the plaintiffs at the Los Angeles District Court and the 9th Circuit Court of California. The U.S. Supreme Court later declined to hear the case, effectively upholding the district court's decision to dismiss the lawsuit (Constante, 2017a).

In 2017, a "comfort women" memorial (*"Comfort Women" Column of Strength* by Steven Whyte) was unveiled in the City of San Francisco, and it officially became a city asset. In response, the mayor of Osaka severed the city's 60-year-long sister city relationship with San Francisco (Constante, 2017b).

In 2018, Japan's newly appointed ambassador to the United States, Shinsuke Sugiyama, publicly stated that he intended to visit U.S. cities that have "comfort women" memorials to persuade officials to remove them (Nikkei Asia, 2018).

The Japanese government also pressured other countries to dismantle "comfort women" statues. In 2018, a "comfort women" statue in Manila commemorating Filipino women forced into sexual slavery by the Japanese military mysteriously disappeared overnight from a major city road— allegedly due to Japanese pressure on the government of the Philippines (Varona, 2019). The statue was later returned to the artist, but it was subsequently stolen from his residence, and its whereabouts remain unknown (Manahan, 2018). Even a statue installed on private property in the Philippines was removed without explanation (Jung, 2019).

In 2022, Prime Minister Fumio Kishida requested German Chancellor Olaf Scholz's assistance in removing the *Statue of Peace* in Berlin. Chancellor Scholz declined, stating that the matter fell under the local government's jurisdiction (Cho, 2022). In May 2024, Berlin Mayor Kai Wegner hinted at removing the statue after a meeting with a Japanese diplomat (The Berliner, 2024). Since then, the City of Berlin ordered the civic group responsible for installing the statue to remove it or face a heavy fine. As of this book's publication, local residents continue to fight to keep the memorial.

Attempting to Remove "Comfort Women" from U.S. History Textbooks

A significant event in 2015 involved the U.S. textbook publisher McGraw Hill, which publicly rejected an uninvited demand from the Japanese government to revise or delete passages about "comfort women" in one of its high school Advanced Placement textbooks. The textbook's author refused to comply, and the incident led to widespread condemnation of the Japanese government from U.S. academics, who criticized the attempts to revise history (Fifield, 2015; Martin, 2015).

Applying Political Obstruction at UNESCO

In 2015, 14 organizations from eight countries formed an international committee to nominate historical documents related to "comfort women" for inclusion in the UNESCO's Memory of the World Register. Since then, the Japanese government has actively obstructed the process, even threatening to withdraw from UNESCO, leveraging its status as the organization's most prominent financial contributor (after the United States) to apply pressure (Cho, 2017). As of this book's publication, the joint application to register 2,744 documents remains pending.

17

Teaching Conflict-Related Sexual Violence Through Human Rights Education:
The Case of the Japanese Military's "Comfort Women"

2015 Japan–South Korea Agreement

On December 28, 2015, the Japanese and South Korean foreign ministers announced at a joint press conference that the "comfort women" issue had been "finally and irreversibly" resolved through an apology and financial support (1 billion yen, approximately $8.3 million) from the Japanese government (Ministry of Foreign Affairs of Japan, 2015). However, no signed document was produced to formalize these statements.

International media initially hailed the deal as a breakthrough in the historically fraught relationship between South Korea and Japan. However, survivors and advocacy groups immediately rejected the deal due to several critical flaws (Hosaka, 2021):

1. Exclusion of Survivors: The victims were entirely excluded from the negotiation process.
2. Lack of Legal Accountability: The Japanese government did not acknowledge legal responsibility for violating international laws.
3. Denial of Legal Compensation: After announcing the deal, the Japanese government clarified that the financial support was not legal compensation and should not be interpreted as an admission of guilt.
4. Exclusion of Victims from Other Countries: The agreement only applied to South Korean survivors, leaving the victims from other countries unrecognized.
5. Gag Order on South Korea: The deal included a provision preventing the South Korean government from raising the issue in international forums, including the United Nations.
6. Call for the Removal of the *Statue of Peace*: The agreement urged South Korea to remove the *Statue of Peace* in front of the Japanese Embassy in Seoul, which was widely seen as an attempt to erase historical memory.

Due to widespread public opposition, the agreement began to unravel in 2017. As a result, the Reconciliation and Healing Foundation, established under the deal to administer the fund to survivors, was officially dissolved (Kang, 2018).

History Revisionism in Academia

Like the denials of other atrocities, history revisionism on the "comfort women" issue extends beyond the political sphere and into academia. In recent years, several scholars and journalists from Japan, the United States, and South Korea have contributed to this effort, challenging established historical accounts.

One of the most prominent cases is that of Mark Ramseyer, a professor at Harvard Law School, whose controversial 2021 paper denied that the "comfort women" system constituted sexual slavery (Ramseyer, 2021). He argued, using game theory, that all Korean "comfort women" were voluntary prostitutes under contractual agreements rather than victims of trickery or coercion. However, his claims ignored extensive historical evidence, including survivor testimonies, the 1993 Kono Statement, and multiple UN reports that classify the system as a crime against humanity. Historians and scholars across disciplines widely condemned his work as historical revisionism, noting that he failed to provide a single actual contract or credible sources to substantiate his claims

18

Teaching Conflict-Related Sexual Violence Through Human Rights Education:
The Case of the Japanese Military's "Comfort Women"

(Binkley, 2021; Dudden, 2021; Gersen, 2021; Min, 2025; Yoshimi, 2022). The academic journal that published his article later issued an Expression of Concern (2021).

An Ongoing Problem

Despite repeatedly stating that it upholds the Kono Statement, the Japanese government has consistently taken measures that contradict its fundamental message. While the Kono Statement acknowledges the Japanese military's direct involvement in the coercion and suffering of "comfort women" and promises to face the history, subsequent administrations—particularly under former Prime Minister Shinzo Abe and his successors—have taken measures that directly contradict it by attempting to revise school textbooks, pressure foreign governments to remove memorials, and obstruct international recognition of historical records.

Japan's dual strategy allows it to claim continuity in its official position while simultaneously erasing historical accountability through diplomatic and political maneuvers. While publicly upholding the Kono Statement, the Abe administration questioned key aspects of its content, such as the extent of coercion. Additionally, Japan's official diplomacy asserts that it has expressed "sincere apologies" for the "comfort women" issue (Ministry of Foreign Affairs of Japan, 2015, para. 2), yet its representatives have consistently denied legal responsibility, arguing that all reparations were settled through postwar treaties. This obfuscation pattern confuses international audiences and frustrates victims and advocacy groups seeking an unambiguous acknowledgment of historical wrongdoing.

19

Teaching Conflict-Related Sexual Violence Through Human Rights Education:
The Case of the Japanese Military's "Comfort Women"

Lesson Plan: *Historical Contentions on "Comfort Women"*

Description
This lesson teaches about the denial of the "comfort women" history. Featured teaching strategies include small group work and discussions, whole class discussions, testimony analysis, and political cartoon analysis.

Objectives
By the end of this lesson, students will be able to
- explain why the Japanese government's denial of the "comfort women" history is baseless and
- tie the denial of the "comfort women" history to the human rights framework.

NCSS Themes
❷ TIME, CONTINUITY, AND CHANGE
❺ INDIVIDUALS, GROUPS, AND INSTITUTIONS

Sources
- Source A: Part 5 of Section 2, "The Comfort Women Issue in the International Community," from *Japan's Efforts on the Issue of Comfort Women*, by the Ministry of Foreign Affairs of Japan (**www.mofa.go.jp/policy/postwar/page22e_000883. html**)
- Source B: Statement of Jan Ruff-O'Herne at the House of Representatives Hearing on Protecting the Human Rights of "Comfort Women," February 15, 2007 (**https://web.archive.org/web/20160303152117/http://archives. republicans.foreignaffairs.house.gov/110/ohe021507.htm**)
- Source C: Testimony of Zhou Fenying from *Chinese Comfort Women: Testimonies From Imperial Japan's Sex Slaves* (p. 89–93), by Peipei Qiu, 2013, Oxford University Press. If teachers do not have access to this book, they can download the free *Curriculum and Resources Handbook* in the Lesson Plans section of the Comfort Women Education website (**https://comfortwomeneducation.org**). An excerpt of Zhang's testimony can be found on page 38 of this handbook.
- Source D: "'Comfort Women:' The Contention of Historical Narrative," by J. Williams and B. Cha, 2023, *Oregon Journal of the Social Studies*, 11(2), pp. 96–116 (**https://sites.google.com/site/oregoncouncilforsocialstudies/O-J-S-S/o-j-s-s-issues**)

Lesson Activities (45 minutes)
Opening Discussion (5 minutes)
Open the discussion with *Last class, we learned about the history of "comfort women." Who can define "comfort women"?* Wait for students' responses. *That is very good! Today, let's continue learning about the "comfort women" issue. First, I'd like to show you a quotation from Japan's*

20

Teaching Conflict-Related Sexual Violence Through Human Rights Education:
The Case of the Japanese Military's "Comfort Women"

former Prime Minister Shinzo Abe. Project the following quotation on the board in front of the classroom:

> What is the purpose of teaching the pure and innocent children fabricated lies (by China and South Korea) about "300,000 massacred in Nanjing" or "Forced sexual slavery of the comfort women"? ... It only serves to make the children disillusioned by their country, hate their ancestors and become ashamed of their evil conducts. That will lead to an even more horrifying outcome. It will rob them of a sense of pride to live as worthy individuals. (as cited in Shibata, 2013, p. 77)

Ask students, *What was Abe trying to say? What is your reaction to this quotation?* Call for volunteers to share their answers.

Mini-Lecture (5 minutes)
1. The Japanese government has been denying certain aspects of the history of "comfort women." Teachers can find the content for this mini-lecture in Source A.
2. The three aspects of "comfort women" denial are as follows:
    a. There was no coercion, or they were not forcibly taken.
    b. They were not "sex slaves."
    c. The total number of 200,000 is baseless.

Document Analysis (20 minutes)
1. Put students into small groups of three or four. Randomly assign the testimonies of Jan Ruff-O'Herne, a Dutch survivor (Source B), or Zhou Fenying, a Chinese survivor (Source C).
2. After reading their respective testimony, each group will discuss the same questions:
    a. How did the victim become a "comfort woman"?
    b. Did they have freedom when they were in the "comfort stations"?
    c. Based on the testimony, how do you evaluate the Japanese government's standpoints, that "comfort women" were "not forcibly taken" and that they were "not sex slaves"?
    d. Ask each group to share their answers.
3. Wrap up the activity: *The testimonies are strong evidence that there were "comfort women" who were forcibly taken, regardless of nationality or ethnicity, and that they were sex slaves and completely stripped of freedom while inside the "comfort station" system. In terms of the numbers of "comfort women," it is hard to tell because the Imperial Japanese Army destroyed most of the military documents at the end of the war. However, Japanese and Chinese historians estimate that hundreds of thousands of women and girls became victims (Qiu, 2013; Yoshimi, 1995).*

Political Cartoon Analysis (10 minutes)
Figure 2.1 *Comfort Whitewash*

Note. From "Comfort Whitewash," by Roger Dahl, *The Japan Times*, March 21, 2015. Copyright by Roger Dahl. Reprinted with permission.

Show the "Comfort Whitewash" political cartoon (Figure 2.1) and ask the following questions:
- What do you notice first?
- List the people and objects in the cartoon.
- Who is the man? What is he trying to do? What is he saying?
- Which of the visuals are symbols?
- What do they stand for?
- What words or phrases are the most significant? Why?
- Who drew this cartoon?
- Where was the cartoon published?
- What is the message the cartoonist wants to send? What led you to your conclusion?
- What questions do you have for the cartoonist? How can you find the answers?

Exit Ticket (5 minutes)
Hand out the exit ticket with the following questions:
- What do you think of the Japanese government's denial of "comfort women"?
- Do you consider the denial a continued violation of these women's human rights?

22

Teaching Conflict-Related Sexual Violence Through Human Rights Education:
The Case of the Japanese Military's "Comfort Women"

Assessments

1. Testimony Analysis: Students will be assessed through the teacher's observation during small group and whole class discussions as they analyze the testimonies.
2. Exit Ticket: Give students a piece of paper and have them write down their answers to the two questions listed in the lesson plan.

Accommodation

If a student has a vision impairment, the teacher should print out the political cartoon and give it to the student before the political cartoon analysis activity.

Extension Activities

Teachers can use documentaries to show the historical contention on the "comfort women" issue. Williams and Cha (2023; Source D) designed a lesson plan to demonstrate how to teach this issue through *Shusenjo: Comfort Women and Japan's War on History*, a documentary that contains the deniers' narratives and the supporters' counternarratives. The lesson plan is available open access.

Teaching Conflict-Related Sexual Violence Through Human Rights Education:
The Case of the Japanese Military's "Comfort Women"

Chapter 3. The Responses

But my life has been shaped by events beyond my control, above all the wars since 1996 that have ravaged Congo, and women in particular, under the mostly indifferent gaze of the rest of the world. (Mukwege, 2021, p. xiii)

International Responses to Conflict-Related Sexual Violence

Throughout much of history, sexual violence has been regarded as "a private matter," with victims often being blamed for their experiences (Barstow, 2000, p. 234). In such an environment, women who have endured conflict-related sexual violence (CRSV) usually choose to remain silent (Jacob, 2020; Ruff-O'Herne, 2008). Due to the silence, the true extent of wartime sexual violence has been frequently overlooked or ignored by society and authorities. Victims are often left without support, while the perpetrators rarely face justice. The stigma surrounding sexual violence, combined with social pressures to conform to traditional gender roles, further isolates survivors, making it difficult for them to seek help or speak out (Trial International, 2020). This silence perpetuates cycles of violence, marginalizing women's experiences in historical narratives and wartime accounts. The following section highlights key moments in history when the international community came together in response to the sexual violence against women in armed conflicts.

Early Legal Recognition of Conflict-Related Sexual Violence

It was not until the large-scale mass rapes and systematic sexual enslavement of women during the early 1990s conflict in Bosnia and Herzegovina that international legal attention began to focus on war crimes against women (Henry, 2011). In January 1993, the United Nations (UN) Human Rights Commission identified rape as a war crime for the first time (Rittner & Roth, 2012). Shortly after, in May 1993, the UN passed Resolution 827, establishing the International Criminal Tribunal for the former Yugoslavia (ICTY) in the Hague, the Netherlands. The following year, in November 1994, the UN Security Council adopted Resolution 955, creating the International Criminal Tribunal for Rwanda (ICTR) in Arusha, Tanzania. However, both courts struggled to prosecute conflict-related sexual violence effectively. As Barstow (2000) explains,

> They could neither compel nations to hand over accused persons nor hand down the death penalty. As such, they had far less power than the Nuremberg and Tokyo courts had had. And they had an insufficient grasp of what would be involved in trying sexual crimes. As a result, the trials began at an agonizingly slow pace. (p. 241)

The first trial charging rape at ICTY did not occur until 1998 (Barstow, 2000). By 2011, the ICTY had indicted 161 individuals, with only 28 convicted for committing sexual violence. Meanwhile, ICTR convicted just 11 perpetrators for CRSV during the Rwandan genocide (Rittner & Roth, 2012).

International Conferences and Advocacy Efforts

In August 1995, the Fourth World Conference on Women was held in Beijing, China, with over

24

Teaching Conflict-Related Sexual Violence Through Human Rights Education: The Case of the Japanese Military's "Comfort Women"

50,000 delegates from 189 countries. The conference adopted resolutions addressing CRSV against women, explicitly recognizing rape in armed conflicts as a war crime and condemning the practice of blaming women for sexual violence committed against them (UN, 1995).

Five years later, the UN General Assembly held the Beijing +5 special session to review the progress of the 1995 Beijing Declaration and Platform for Action. At this session, the Secretary-General formally acknowledged women's human rights, emphasizing that sexual violence against women was illegal (UN, 2000).

In June 2006, the first International Symposium on Sexual Violence in Conflict and Beyond (hereafter, Symposium) was held in Brussels, Belgium (United Nations Population Fund, 2006). The participants issued the Brussels Call to Action, calling for "urgent and long-term action" to prevent and respond to sexual violence in conflict (Symposium, 2006, p. 2).

Following the Symposium, the UN Action Against Sexual Violence in Conflict (hereafter, UN Action) was established in 2007. This initiative became a key force within the UN for addressing CRSV. Through its advocacy, the UN Security Council passed several landmark resolutions, including the following:

- Resolution 1820 (2008), which for the first time, recognized wartime sexual violence as a war crime and a threat to global peace and security, demanding an immediate end to such acts (UN Security Council, 2008).
- Resolutions 1888 (2009), 1960 (2010), 2106 (2013), 2332 (2016), and 2467 (2019) strengthened measures to combat sexual violence in conflict (UN Action, n.d.; UN Security Council, 2009).

In 2020, UN Action adopted its Strategic Framework (2020–2025), shifting the focus from impunity to deterrence. This framework emphasized addressing the root causes of gender inequality in both wartime and peacetime while promoting a survivor-centered approach (UN Action, 2020).

The Persistent Challenge: Calls for Action

Looking back to the past three decades, the international community has made progress in raising awareness and advocating for solutions to CRSV. However, much work remains. Many nations continue to ignore these atrocities.

In 2018, Nobel Peace Prize laureate Nadia Murad, a Yazidi survivor of ISIS sexual slavery, expressed her deep frustration with the inaction of the international community. She reflects on the genocide and enslavement of Yazidi women and girls in her Nobel Prize lecture:

> If justice is not done, this genocide will be repeated against us and against other vulnerable communities.... My community has been subjected to genocide for more than four years. The international community did nothing to deter it nor to stop it. It did not bring the perpetrators to justice. (Murad, 2018, paras. 19, 21)

That same year, fellow Nobel Peace Prize laureate Dr. Denis Mukwege, a Congolese gynecologist, echoed Murad's frustration. Having spent decades treating survivors of sexual violence at Panzi Hospital in the Democratic Republic of Congo (DRC), Mukwege passionately declared in his Nobel Prize lecture, "The Congolese people have been humiliated, abused and massacred for more than two decades in plain sight of the international community" (Mukwege, 2018, para. 41).

Both Murad and Mukwege called for meaningful actions to hold perpetrators accountable. Mukwege urged, "Taking action means saying 'no' to indifference. If there is a war to be waged, it is the war against the indifference which is eating away at our societies" (Mukwege, 2018, paras. 82–83)

Ongoing Violence and the Urgency for Action

As you read this book, sexual violence in conflict zones persists. On January 26, 2025, Goma, the largest city in the eastern DRC, fell to the Rwandan-backed M23 rebel group, resulting in nearly 3,000 deaths and thousands of injuries in just the first week of conflict (UN, 2025). Sexual violence has been widespread as the armed conflict escalates (Women's Initiatives for Gender Justice, 2025). On February 15, 2025, M23 entered Bukavu, the second-largest city in the eastern DRC (Makumeno, 2025). This city is home to Dr. Mukwege's Panzi Hospital.

On February 19, 2025, Dr. Mukwege voiced his outrage in an interview with *The New York Times*, stating, "A bloody conflict is met with condemnations but no meaningful action. This stark contrast is not just neglect; it is selective justice" (Mukwege, 2025, para. 1). Since 1999, Panzi Hospital has treated over 83,000 survivors of sexual violence, 30% of whom were children (Mukwege, 2025).

With sexual violence in conflict zones continuing to devastate lives, what can the international community do? Condemnations and symbolic resolutions are not enough. Words alone will not bring justice. As we move forward, we must ask ourselves: How can we turn awareness into action?

In the next section, we will examine how the international community has responded to the Japanese military's "comfort women" issue. This section will conclude with a 45-minute lesson plan about these reactions.

International Responses to the "Comfort Women" Issue

Since the 1990s, the international community, including the UN and several national governments, has taken significant steps to respond to the "comfort women" survivors' call for justice. Key international responses include UN reports, international resolutions, and ongoing efforts to ensure accountability and historical justice.

Early UN Reports and Findings

After Hak-sun Kim made the historic testimony in 1991 and after the subsequent testimonies by "comfort women" survivors from other countries, international organizations, particularly the UN, began scrutinizing Japan's responsibility for wartime atrocities. Two pivotal reports by UN Special Rapporteurs played a critical role in shaping the international legal and human rights discourse.

In 1996, Radhika Coomaraswamy, the UN Special Rapporteur on Violence Against Women, issued a landmark report that categorized Japan's wartime sexual slavery system as a crime against humanity. The report urged Japan to resolve the issue by carrying out six recommendations: (1) accept full legal responsibility, (2) pay compensation to individual victims, (3) fully disclose military documents and materials, (4) make a public apology, (5) raise awareness of these issues by teaching the historical realities, and (6) identify and punish the perpetrators (UN Economic and Social Council, 1996). Coomaraswamy stressed that the issue was not only about historical recognition but also about Japan's obligation under international law.

In 1998, the UN issued another special report, the 1998 McDougall Report. The findings of

26

Teaching Conflict-Related Sexual Violence Through Human Rights Education:
The Case of the Japanese Military's "Comfort Women"

Gay J. McDougall, the UN Special Rapporteur on Contemporary Forms of Slavery, reinforced Coomaraswamy's conclusions, emphasizing that the forced sexual slavery system was equivalent to enslavement and systematic rape under international law. The report also argued that Japan's domestic compensation mechanisms were insufficient and recommended a state-sponsored reparations program (UN Economic and Social Council, 1998).

Women's International War Crimes Tribunal on Japan's Military Sexual Slavery
In December 2000, the Women's International War Crimes Tribunal on Japan's Military Sexual Slavery was convened in Tokyo by an international coalition of human rights organizations and legal experts. Although it was a people's tribunal without legal enforcement power, the event was significant in bringing global attention to Japan's wartime atrocities. The tribunal found Emperor Hirohito and other Japanese military and political leaders guilty of crimes against humanity for their role in the "comfort women" system. The proceedings and verdict, though symbolic, reinforced the demand for justice and set a precedent for addressing wartime sexual violence in international human rights discourse (Arumugham & Ying, 2024; KYEOL, 2025).

European Parliament and Other Nation's Resolutions
The European Parliament passed a similar resolution to the U.S. House Resolution 121 (discussed later in this section) in 2007, urging Japan to take full responsibility and provide reparations (European Parliament, 2007). Similar resolutions were adopted by the national legislatures of the Netherlands, Canada, and South Korea, demonstrating global solidarity with the victims (Women's Active Museum on War and Peace, n.d.-b). In addition to these national resolutions, numerous city resolutions were passed in Japan and other cities in Australia, the United States, and South Korea.

International Criticism of the 2015 Japan–South Korea Agreement
In 2015, Japan and South Korea reached an agreement intended to "finally and irreversibly" resolve the "comfort women" issue (Ministry of Foreign Affairs of Japan, 2015). This agreement faced intense criticism from victims and international human rights bodies, as it did not involve direct consultation with survivors and lacked an explicit acknowledgment of Japan's legal responsibility.

The UN Committee on the Elimination of Discrimination Against Women (CEDAW) criticized the 2015 Japan–South Korea Agreement for failing to fully respect victims' rights. CEDAW found the resolution provided by Japan's delegation relating to the "comfort women" issue unacceptable and contradictory and urged Japan to ensure that any resolution was in line with international human rights standards and included full recognition of state responsibility, comprehensive reparations, and historical education initiatives (UN Human Rights, 2016).

Recent UN Human Rights Report on Japan
Despite diplomatic efforts, the UN and other human rights organizations have continued to highlight Japan's inadequate and contradictory response to the "comfort women" issue. In 2022, the concluding observations on the seventh periodic report of Japan from the UN Human Rights Committee under the International Covenant on Civil and Political Rights emphasized that Japan has not fulfilled its obligations to truthfully address historical injustices or provide adequate reparations (UN International Covenant on Civil and Political Rights, 2022). The committee noted

Japan's lack of progress in implementing previous recommendations and expressed regret that Japan continues to deny its obligation to address the ongoing human rights violations experienced by the victims. It criticized the absence of criminal investigations, prosecutions, and effective remedies, including full reparations to victims. The committee called on Japan to take immediate and effective legislative and administrative measures to ensure (a) independent and impartial investigations into all allegations of human rights violations against "comfort women," disclosure of all available evidence, and prosecution of perpetrators; (b) justice and complete reparations for all victims and their families, including those from abroad; and (c) education on this matter, with accurate depictions in textbooks and a firm rejection of any efforts to tarnish victims or deny historical truths (UN International Covenant on Civil and Political Rights, 2022).

Legislative and Diplomatic Response from the United States

Following the UN reports by the Special Rapporteurs in 1996 and 1998, the U.S. federal and state governments adopted resolutions urging Japan to take greater responsibility for the "comfort women" issue. These resolutions reflected a global consensus on the need for Japan to provide a sincere apology and proper restitution.

One of the most significant responses came from the U.S. House of Representatives—House Resolution 121 in 2007. This resolution called on Japan to formally acknowledge and apologize unequivocally for its wartime sexual slavery system. It also urged Japan to educate future generations about this history to prevent recurrence (H.R. Resolution 121, 2007).

In addition to the 2007 resolution, several city and state resolutions across the United States have been adopted to support and honor the victims of the "comfort women" system. The New York State Senate adopted Resolution J304 in 2013, memorializing a monument in the state that pays tribute to the "comfort women." The resolution recognized the suffering endured by these women and emphasized the importance of acknowledging this history to prevent future crimes against humanity (N.Y. Sen. Resolution J304, 2013).

On September 22, 2015, the San Francisco Board of Supervisors (SF Board) unanimously passed Resolution 342-15, urging the establishment of a memorial dedicated to the "comfort women" and promoting education to combat global human trafficking of women and girls (SF Board Resolution 342-15, 2015). The memorial, known as the *"Comfort Women" Column of Strength*, was unveiled on September 22, 2017. On April 6, 2021, the SF Board unanimously passed Resolution 151–21, denouncing Harvard Law Professor J. Mark Ramseyer's article "Contracting for Sex in the Pacific War" (SF Board Resolution 151-21, 2021). The resolution reaffirmed support for "comfort women" and condemned efforts to deny historical atrocities ("Comfort Women" Justice Coalition, 2021).

Conclusion

The international community has played a crucial role in advocating for justice for "comfort women" victims. UN reports, legislative resolutions, and diplomatic efforts have repeatedly called for Japan to accept full responsibility and ensure comprehensive reparations. However, despite these efforts, Japan's response has often been criticized as insufficient. Moving forward, Japan must engage in a survivor-centered approach, acknowledge its legal responsibilities, and uphold the principles of historical justice to provide closure to the victims and their families. Until these steps are taken, the call for justice will persist on the global stage.

28

Teaching Conflict-Related Sexual Violence Through Human Rights Education:
The Case of the Japanese Military's "Comfort Women"

Lesson Plan: *International Community Reaction to the "Comfort Women" Issue*

Description
This lesson explores how the international community has responded to the Japanese military "comfort women" issue. Key teaching strategies include small group discussions, document analysis, research, peer teaching, and group presentations.

Objectives
By the end of this lesson, students will be able to
- describe various international responses to Japan's denial of the "comfort women" issue;
- analyze how different countries, organizations, and individuals have advocated for the recognition and justice for the "comfort women"; and
- engage in discussions on the significance of historical recognition and its global political ramifications.

NCSS Themes
❺ INDIVIDUALS, GROUPS, AND INSTITUTIONS
❿ CIVIC IDEALS AND PRACTICES

Sources
- Source A: UN Report of the Special Rapporteur, 1996 (**https://digitallibrary. un.org/record/228137?v=pdf**)
- Source B: United States House Resolution 121, 110th Congress, 2007 (**www. congress.gov/bill/110th-congress/house-resolution/121/text**)
- Source C: "Why Did the 2015 Japan-Korea 'Comfort Women' Agreement Fall Apart?" by Y. Hosaka, 2021, *The Diplomat* (**https://thediplomat.com/2021/11/ why-did-the-2015-japan-korea-comfort-women-agreement-fall-apart**). *Note to teachers*: Depending on time, teachers may use excerpts instead of the whole article.

Lesson Activities (45 minutes)
Brief Recap (5 minutes)
- Ask students to recall what they already know about the history of the "comfort women" issue. Pose the following discussion questions:
  - What do you remember about the history of the Japanese military "comfort women"?
  - What is the Japanese government's current stance on this issue?
- Transition: Ask students to predict how other countries and international organizations might have responded to Japan's denial, highlighting the issue's ongoing international significance.

Mini-Lecture: Overview of International Responses (10 minutes)
Provide a brief lecture on key international responses:
- **United Nations**: Discuss the UN's stance, including the 1996 report by the UN Commission on Human Rights and their call for Japan to take responsibility and the varying reactions to Japan's refusal.
- **United States**: Examine House Resolution 121 and its significance.
- **South Korea**: Analyze South Korea's diplomatic initiatives and public campaigns for justice, including the 2015 Japan–South Korea agreement and the controversy surrounding it.
- **International Media Coverage**: Highlight how global media has reported on the issue and the impact of this coverage.

Distribute a handout summarizing these responses (see Sources A–C).

Group Activity: Analyzing International Responses (15 minutes)
1. Divide the class into small groups (3–4 students per group).
2. Assign each group a source (see above) to read and research.
3. Provide guiding questions to facilitate analysis:
    - What is the official position of this article regarding Japan's denial of the "comfort women" issue?
    - How has this article advocated for recognition and justice?
    - What challenges or criticisms have they faced?
4. Groups research and discuss their assigned topic using handouts, online resources, or class materials.

Group Presentations (10 minutes)
1. Each group presents their findings in a two-minute summary.
2. Encourage engaging presentations using visuals, quotations, or key statistics.

Five-Minute Journaling (5 minutes): Ask students to write a short reflection beginning with "It is important for the international community to respond to historical injustices like the 'comfort women' issue because...."

Assessments
1. Group Discussions and Presentations: The teacher will observe students' learning through observation during group discussion and their presentations.
2. Five-Minute Journal Reflections: The teacher will assess the content of students' reflections.

Accommodations
- If a student has learning disabilities (e.g., dyslexia, ADHD), the teacher can provide audio versions of the sources or allow text-to-speech tools and offer

Teaching Conflict-Related Sexual Violence Through Human Rights Education:
The Case of the Japanese Military's "Comfort Women"

extended reading and processing time.
- If a student is an English language learner (ELL), the teacher can simplify language, provide translated key terms, use visual aids, or pair ELL students with a peer mentor.
- If a student has a visual impairment, the teacher can offer enlarged print or Braille handouts of the sources, ensure screen reader compatibility for digital materials, and provide detailed verbal descriptions of visuals.
- If a student is gifted, the teacher can encourage independent research on additional international responses not covered in class, allow them to take on leadership roles during group activities, and challenge them with a deeper analysis, such as comparing international responses to similar historical injustices.

Extension Activities

Encourage students to compare international responses to the "comfort women" issue with other historical injustices, evaluating global approaches to justice and reconciliation. Suggested topics include the following:
- The Holocaust: post–World War II reparations and recognition efforts
- The Rwandan Genocide: the role of the International Criminal Tribunal for Rwanda (ICTR)
- Native American History: the long struggle for recognition and reparations in the United States
- The Armenian Genocide: international recognition efforts and political challenges

*Teaching Conflict-Related Sexual Violence Through Human Rights Education:
The Case of the Japanese Military's "Comfort Women"*

Part II. Learning for Human Rights

Human rights education is much more than a lesson in schools or a theme for a day; it is a process to equip people with the tools they need to live lives of security and dignity.

—Kofi Annan,
former United Nations Secretary-General,
2001 Nobel Peace Prize Winner

Human rights education without action is futile. After learning about human rights, the next step is to apply the knowledge and take action, fighting against injustices. Brander and colleagues (2023) suggest some simple actions for human rights: (a) engaging in public actions, such as protests, petitions, or sit-ins, to raise awareness of an issue and get the media's attention; (b) encouraging young people to educate their peers; (c) doing it yourself; (d) changing the policy or behavior of state representatives; (e) collaborating with other groups or movements; and (f) gathering evidence.

Survivors of conflict-related sexual violence (CRSV), activists, and nongovernment organizations in different countries are still fighting for justice for the victims. The second part of this book brings attention to the resistance movements and the ways people memorialize the victims of CRSV worldwide, using the Japanese military's "comfort women" system as a case study for teaching purposes.

32

Teaching Conflict-Related Sexual Violence Through Human Rights Education:
The Case of the Japanese Military's "Comfort Women"

Chapter 4. The Resistance

Japan continues to do nothing but lie and say outrageous things. I don't know how long we're going to have to wait [for an apology], but I plan to keep it up until then.

—Yong-soo Lee,
a survivor of the Japanese military's
"comfort woman" system

Confronting Conflict-Related Sexual Violence Worldwide

International responses to conflict-related sexual violence (CRSV), as discussed in Chapter 3, represent one approach to addressing the issue. This chapter examines additional methods of resistance, including survivor advocacy, legal actions, international sanctions and diplomatic pressure, and survivor support.

Survivor Advocacy

Activists and nonprofit organizations worldwide are crucial in raising awareness about CRSV and advocating for justice. In Sarajevo, Bosnia and Herzegovina, the Association of Women Victims of War fights for the rights of women subjected to rape and other war crimes during the Bosnian War (1992–1995). The organization has led protests and awareness campaigns demanding justice and recognition for survivors (Sarajevo Times, 2023).

The South Sudan Women's Empowerment Network (SSWEN)—a nonprofit, nonpartisan, and nongovernmental organization founded in 2005—works to improve the lives of women in South Sudan, including educating communities about the consequences of CRSV. Part of SSWEN's advocacy raises awareness of and supports those who experience sexual violence as a result of child abuse in schools, commercial sex, girl compensation, forced and child marriage, rape, and human trafficking (SSWEN, n.d.). Activists and survivors of sexual violence in South Sudan continue to demand justice and reparations (Amnesty International, 2017).

In the Democratic Republic of the Congo and Uganda, the Women's Initiatives for Gender Justice (WIGJ) has been a leading force in advancing women's rights. This international human rights organization works toward gender equality and justice through partnerships with the International Criminal Court and grassroots organizations (WIGJ, n.d.).

Legal Actions

Legal mechanisms have played a pivotal role in addressing CRSV. In 1998, the International Criminal Tribunal for Rwanda set a historic precedent by convicting Jean-Paul Akayesu of rape as a crime against humanity and genocide. This was the first instance in which an international court recognized sexual violence as an act of genocide (UN International Residual Mechanism for Criminal Tribunals, 1998).

Following the Bosnian War (1992–1995), during which an estimated 20,000–50,000 women were raped, the International Criminal Tribunal for the former Yugoslavia prosecuted wartime

33

Teaching Conflict-Related Sexual Violence Through Human Rights Education:
The Case of the Japanese Military's "Comfort Women"

sexual violence as a crime against humanity. A landmark case in 2001, *Kunarac et al.*, established an important legal precedent (UN International Residual Mechanism for Criminal Tribunals, n.d.).

The International Criminal Court has also held perpetrators accountable for war crimes involving sexual violence. In 2019, Congolese warlord Bosco Ntaganda, leader of the Patriotic Forces for the Liberation of Congo militia, was convicted of rape, sexual slavery, and the conscription of child soldiers. He was sentenced to 30 years in prison. Similarly, in 2021, Dominic Ongwen, a former commander of the Lord's Resistance Army, was convicted of crimes including forced pregnancy, forced marriage, rape, and sexual enslavement in Uganda, receiving a 25-year sentence.

International Sanctions and Diplomatic Pressure

To combat CRSV, the international community has imposed sanctions and diplomatic pressure on perpetrator nations. In 2017, the Myanmar military committed widespread sexual violence against Rohingya women and girls during the Rohingya genocide. In response, the European Union (EU) and the United States imposed targeted sanctions on Myanmar's top military officials (EU, 2018; U.S. Department of the Treasury, 2018). These sanctions remain in place, enforced by the EU, the UK, and the US (Global Sanctions, n.d.).

Beyond Myanmar, the US and EU have also imposed sanctions on South Sudan, Syria, Russia, Sudan, and Eritrea for their involvement in CRSV.

Survivor Support

Supporting survivors of CRSV takes various forms, including medical, psychological, and legal aid. A notable example is the Panzi Hospital in the Democratic Republic of the Congo, founded in 1999 by Dr. Denis Mukwege, recipient of the 2018 Nobel Peace Prize. The hospital provides surgical and psychological care to survivors of CRSV and offers legal assistance and reintegration programs, serving as a global model for comprehensive survivor support (Panzi, n.d.). In Rwanda, the Association des Veuves du Génocide (Association of Widows of Genocide, AVEGA), founded by 50 widowed survivors of the 1994 Rwandan genocide, provides holistic support to women and children affected by the conflict (n.d.).

Some countries have also served as resettlement destinations and safe havens for survivors of CRSV. During the ISIS genocide against the Yazidi community in Iraq in 2014, thousands of women and girls were subjected to sexual slavery and violence. In response, Germany established a special refugee quota for Yazidis in 2015 and supported the EU refugee quota program (Frymark, 2015). In 2017, Canada also began accepting Yazidi refugees (Government of Canada, 2017).

The following section will examine the Wednesday Demonstration, the world's longest-running protest, in which South Korean citizens continue to demand justice for survivors of the Japanese military's "comfort women" system.

Wednesday Demonstration: The World's Longest-Running Human Rights Protest

A few months after Hak-sun Kim's groundbreaking public testimony in 1991, Japan announced that Prime Minister Kiichi Miyazawa would visit South Korea. On January 8, 1992, the day of his visit, survivors and supporters gathered in front of the Japanese Embassy in Seoul, South Korea, to protest Japan's continued denial and lack of accountability regarding its wartime sexual slavery system. What began as a single demonstration became a weekly protest, now recognized as the world's longest-running human rights protest (Bemma, 2017; Jang, 2021; The Korean Council for Justice and Remembrance, n.d.). Teachers can find black-and-white photographs of the first Wednesday Demonstration on the website for the South Korean newspaper *Kyunghyang Shinmun* (**www.khan.co.kr/article/201112072153275**).

The Wednesday Demonstration is organized by the Korean Council for Justice and Remembrance for the Issue of Military Sexual Slavery by Japan (hereafter, the Korean Council), formerly known as the Korean Council for the Women Drafted for Military Sexual Slavery by Japan. The Korean Council was founded in 1990 by 37 civic and women's rights organizations in response to growing demands for justice for "comfort women." The protest demands the following actions from the Japanese government:

1. Admit the Japanese military sexual slavery system as a war crime.
2. Disclose official documents.
3. Deliver an official apology.
4. Make reparations to the victims.
5. Punish those responsible.
6. Educate and record the sexual slavery system in history textbooks.
7. Erect a memorial monument and build an official archive. (The Korean Council, n.d.)

Over the years, the protest has been joined by many elderly survivors, activists, students, and supporters from around the world. The movement has gained global attention, inspiring similar campaigns in other countries advocating for historical justice and women's rights. One of the most significant milestones was the 1,000th Wednesday Demonstration on December 14, 2011, which was marked by the unveiling of the *Statue of Peace* in front of the Japanese Embassy in Seoul. Teachers can find photos of the 1,000th demonstration on the Yonhap News Agency website (**www.yna.co.kr/view/AKR20111213093700022**).

Despite persistent pressure from Japan to remove the statue, the protests and memorials continue to stand as a testament to the survivors' fight for justice. The Wednesday Demonstration remains a powerful symbol of resilience, the ongoing struggle for historical justice and women's rights, and a call for Japan to fully acknowledge and take responsibility for its wartime atrocities.

Teaching Conflict-Related Sexual Violence Through Human Rights Education:
The Case of the Japanese Military's "Comfort Women"

Lesson Plan: *Wednesday Demonstration: How Far Are We From Justice?*

Description
This lesson introduces students to the resistance movement against the Japanese military's "comfort women" issue through the Wednesday Demonstration in Seoul, South Korea. Featured teaching strategies include small group work, discussions, peer teaching, and art integration.

Objectives
By the end of this lesson, students will be able to
- explain the Wednesday Demonstration and its historical significance,
- describe the purpose of the demonstrations and why they continue, and
- express support for the "comfort women" survivors by creating a poster that raises awareness.

NCSS Themes
🌑 GLOBAL CONNECTIONS
🌑 CIVIC IDEALS AND PRACTICES

Resources for Group Work 1
- 30 Years of "Comfort Women" Rallies Mark World's Longest Peace Protest, by J. Lee, last modified on August 17, 2022, *Hankyoreh* (**https://english.hani.co.kr/arti/english_edition/e_national/1026300.html**).
- *"Comfort Women" Wednesday Demonstrations: Memory Practices and Troubled Pasts*, by MakingHistories, February 28, 2024 (**www.youtube.com/watch?v=fYjwPDiu8rQ**).
- *Wednesday Demonstration for Resolution of the Issue of Military Sexual Slavery by Japan*, by The Korean Council for Justice and Remembrance for the Issues of Military Sexual Slavery in Japan, (in Korean, English, and Japanese at **https://womenandwar.net/announcement-jpn/?bmode=view&idx=17208499**).
- *Weekly "Wednesday demonstration" Held Peacefully, No Clashes With Far-Right Groups*, by Arirang News, January 19, 2022 (**www.youtube.com/watch?v=Lctm6kqsQjk**).

Lesson Activities (45 minutes)
Opening Discussion (5 minutes)
Begin the discussion with *What are some ways people can express their support for a cause or stand up for justice?* Allow a few students to share responses.

Mini-Lecture: Introduction to the Wednesday Demonstration (5 minutes)
- The **Wednesday Demonstration** refers to a weekly protest in Seoul, South Korea, which has taken place every Wednesday since 1992. It was organized by activists to demand justice for the "comfort women" (women who were forced into sexual slavery by the Japanese military during World War II).

- **Purpose**: The protests aim to pressure the Japanese government to apologize, take responsibility, and compensate the victims.
- **Ongoing Significance**: The demonstrations continue as a way to raise awareness and to ensure that the voices of survivors are heard.

Group Work 1: Deep Dive Into the Issue (15 minutes)

Put students into small groups of three or four. Give students about 10 minutes to further explore and research the Wednesday Demonstration. To better facilitate student research, the teacher may want to consider preparing a list of useful sources (see resources above) for students to read or watch, and then students can look for information using other school-approved websites on their own. Each group will respond to the following:

1. In your own words, define "Wednesday Demonstration" and explain its purpose.
2. Why do you think it is important that these women continue to demand justice, even decades after the events took place?

Group Work 2: Designing a Poster (18 minutes)

Students will design posters that express their support for the survivors of the "comfort women" system and raise awareness about the Wednesday Demonstration. Follow the following guidelines:

- Tell students to imagine they are part of the protest and are making a poster to help spread awareness.
- Ask students to create posters that convey messages of support, justice, and human rights.
- Encourage the use of graphics, symbols, or phrases like "Justice for Comfort Women," "Never Forget," "Stand with Survivors," etc.
- Allow students to use colored markers, pencils, or any available art supplies to create their posters on large paper.

Wrap Up (2 minutes)

- Finish up the poster and put away supplies.
- Inform students that each group will present their posters to the class in the next class period.

Assessments

1. Group Work 1: The teacher will use observation to assess students as they share their answers to the two questions.
2. Group Work 2: The teachers will provide scaffolds to groups as they are working on their posters, using observation to assess students' learning.

Accommodation

If a student has special needs or language barriers, the teacher can group them with students who are supportive, patient, and understanding, as well as those who can help facilitate communication and offer assistance in a collaborative way.

Extension Activities
- Have students research other movements in history where people fought for justice or human rights.
- Organize a class discussion on how different cultures use art and demonstrations to express solidarity.

Chapter 5. The Remembrance

Remembering history is important for us in the present. Even if the Japanese government is uncomfortable with it, the Comfort Women Statue will remain in place for future generations to see.

—Glendale City Council members
(as cited in Choi & Park, 2024, para. 12)

Commemorating Conflict-Related Sexual Violence Worldwide

Conflict-related sexual violence (CRSV) is a harrowing consequence of conflict, and many nations have sought to confront this painful history through commemoration. International and national days of remembrance, memorials, and educational initiatives serve to honor victims and survivors while raising awareness about the widespread impact of such violence. These efforts aim to support survivors, promote accountability, and prevent future atrocities. This section will explore how countries commemorate CRSV and foster a culture of remembrance and justice.

International and National Days of Remembrance

The United Nation (UN) General Assembly designated November 25 as the International Day for the Elimination of Violence Against Women to honor the Mirabal sisters, who were assassinated on this day in 1960 for their opposition to the oppressive regime of Rafael Trujillo in the Dominican Republic. Additionally, December 10 is observed as Human Rights Day to commemorate the adoption of the Universal Declaration of Human Rights in 1948.

In 1991, the Women's Global Leadership Institute, initiated by the Center for Women's Global Leadership at Rutgers University, launched the 16 Days of Activism Against Gender-Based Violence, which runs annually from November 25 to December 10. Since then, the UN has organized numerous public events in conflict-affected regions to raise awareness of gender-based violence (UN Office of the High Commissioner for Human Rights, 2023). For example, in the Democratic Republic of the Congo, people across the country take part in the campaign during the 16 Days of Activism to increase awareness (Mirindi, 2024; Schmitt, 2013).

Other countries have designated specific remembrance days related to CRSV. In Rwanda, the annual genocide commemoration includes events honoring victims and survivors, including those subjected to sexual violence during the 1994 genocide (Republic of Rwanda, 2021).

The South Korean government declared August 14 as the International Memorial Day for Comfort Women in 2017 to honor Hak-sun Kim, the first survivor to publicly testify about her wartime experience as a "comfort woman" (Ministry of Culture, Sports and Tourism, 2021). On this day, various commemorative activities are held across the country.

Memorials and Monuments

Public memorials reflect how we understand history, culture, and identity. They represent what we consider important and embody the collective memory shared and accepted by communities. This is why some statues are erected while others are removed, such as those of Adolf Hitler and Saddam

39

Teaching Conflict-Related Sexual Violence Through Human Rights Education:
The Case of the Japanese Military's "Comfort Women"

Hussein in various parts of the world or Confederate leaders and slave traders in the United States. Memorials serve multiple roles: They honor individuals, events, or groups and provide space for commemoration and remembrance. They also function as tools for history education, reflecting a community or nation's values, struggles, and identity. Many are works of art, adding beauty and significance to public space. Because of their symbolic power, memorials often spark intense debate, strong opposition, and legal challenges.

Memorials and monuments are a part of the fabric of a nation's history and culture. Percoco and Richman (1998) noted that memorials help us reflect on the past and engage our imagination in reevaluating history. While war memorials are common, public memorials rarely commemorate wartime sexual violence (Memorialising Sexual Violence, n.d.). Much like the issue itself, memorials addressing this violence have often been marginalized.

One of the most prominent memorials dedicated to wartime sexual violence is the *Statue of Peace*, which appears in different iterations in cities throughout South Korea to commemorate the victims of the Japanese military's "comfort women" system. Since this statue will be explored in greater depth in the next section, here we highlight several other key wartime sexual violence memorials.

While primarily dedicated to the victims of the Nanjing Massacre (1937–1938), the Memorial Hall of the Victims in Nanjing Massacre by Japanese Invaders also acknowledges the widespread sexual violence committed by the Imperial Japanese Army during the invasion of China. A key component of the Nanjing Massacre Memorial is the site of the Lijixiang Comfort Station, now a museum opened to the public in 2015 (Memorial Hall of the Victims in Nanjing Massacre by Japanese Invaders, n.d.).

In Kosovo, the Heroinat Memorial, unveiled on June 12, 2015, uses 20,000 pins to form the face of an Albanian woman, symbolizing the estimated 20,000 Albanian women raped during the Kosovo War (1998–1999; Howard, 2023; Shehu, 2024).

Education

CRSV education can take different formats, including formal instruction in schools and public education through museums. These efforts vary across countries and are often shaped by the visibility of specific conflicts, the strength of survivor advocacy, and the political willingness to confront difficult histories. In Rwanda, for example, the Kigali Genocide Memorial includes testimonies and exhibits that address sexual violence during the 1994 genocide. In Bosnia and Herzegovina, initiatives such as the Forgotten Children of War project and exhibitions at the War Childhood Museum highlight the experiences of children born of wartime rape. Another prominent example is the Japanese military's "comfort women" system. In South Korea, this history is included in the national curriculum (Cha & Williams, 2025), ensuring that students learn about the experiences of victim-survivors. Beyond the classroom, museums also play a vital role in public education and remembrance. Three prominent institutions in South Korea commemorate and honor victim-survivors while raising awareness of this history: the War and Women's Human Rights Museum in Seoul; the House of Sharing in Gwangju, Gyeonggi-do; and the Heeum Museum of Military Sexual Slavery by Japan in Daegu. In contrast, in Japan—where this history is often downplayed or omitted in textbooks (S. Kim, 2021)—the Women's Active Museum on War and Peace in Tokyo serves as a key educational site.

40

Teaching Conflict-Related Sexual Violence Through Human Rights Education:
The Case of the Japanese Military's "Comfort Women"

In the United States, nonprofit organizations like Comfort Women Action for Redress and Education (CARE) and Comfort Women Justice Coalition (CWJC) work to educate the public about the "comfort women" issue. In 2024, CARE partnered with the Museum of Social Justice in Los Angeles, California, and cohosted an exhibition on the topic (Museum of Social Justice, 2024). From September 2025 to January 2026, CWJC hosted an exhibition in partnership with the main branch of the San Francisco Public Library (CARE, 2025).

"Comfort Women" Statues and Memorials in the United States and the World

Memorials dedicated to the victims of the Japanese military's "comfort women" system are a powerful example of how CRSV is commemorated. These statues and memorials serve as lasting reminders of the suffering endured by the victims and the ongoing fight for justice. Around the world, they stand as symbols of remembrance, activism, and the continued pursuit of historical recognition.

Memorials serve as spaces for remembrance and powerful symbols of activism and resistance. Despite facing opposition and controversy, these monuments ensure that the painful legacy of the "comfort women" system remains publicly acknowledged and never forgotten.

Memorialization Efforts in the United States

Following the 2007 passage of House Resolution 121 that called on Japan to formally acknowledge and apologize for the "comfort women" system, activists sought to raise awareness through public memorials. The first such memorial on public property was established in 2010 at the Palisades Park Public Library in New Jersey. In 2012, Japanese officials attempted to have it removed, but the city refused (Semple, 2012). Following its unveiling, grassroots activism spread rapidly across

Table 5.1 *"Comfort Women" Memorials in the United States*

State	Location
California	Garden Grove, CA Glendale, CA Sonoma State University, CA St. Mary's Square, San Francisco, CA
Connecticut	Korean American Society of Connecticut, Hamden, CT
Georgia	Blackburn Park II, Brookhaven, GA
Michigan	Korean American Cultural Center, Southfield, MI
New Jersey	Bergen County Courthouse, Hackensack, NJ Constitutional Park, Fort Lee, NJ Liberty Plaza, Union City, NJ Palisades Park Public Library, Bergen County, NJ Trinity Episcopal Church, Cliffside Park, NJ
New York	Veterans Memorial, Eisenhower Park, Westbury, NY (There are two "comfort women" memorials in this location.)
Virginia	Fairfax County Government Center, Fairfax, VA

the United States, as activists sought to build more memorials in their cities (P. Kim, 2020). Memorials subsequently emerged across the United States in Bergen County, New Jersey; Glendale, California; Nassau County, New York; Fairfax County, Virginia; Union City, New Jersey; Brookhaven, Georgia; San Francisco, California; and Fort Lee, New Jersey. Others were placed in private locations, including Garden Grove, California; and Southfield, Michigan. Table 5.1 shows the locations of these memorials.

The Statue of Peace *in Seoul, South Korea*

In 2011, during the commemoration of the 1,000th Wednesday Demonstration in front of the Japanese Embassy in Seoul, the Korean Council installed the *Statue of Peace*—a bronze statue of a young girl in traditional Korean dress seated next to an empty chair. She appears to be a teenage girl, her fists clenched and her gaze calm. Surviving Grandmas embraced the statue, saying it reminded them of their younger selves. The monument drew international attention, prompting strong opposition from the Japanese government (Hu, 2017).

The Peace Monument *in Glendale, California*

In 2013, a local community organization, Korean American Forum of California (KAFC), donated the *Peace Monument* to the City of Glendale, California (KAFC, 2013). The statue remains standing today as a powerful symbol of resistance and historical memory, despite fierce opposition from Japanese diplomats and their allies, including a lawsuit that reached the U.S. Supreme Court, where the Japanese government submitted an amicus brief, arguing that removing the memorial from Glendale's park was a matter of Japan's "national core interest" (Zhu, 2017).

The "Comfort Women" Column of Strength *in San Francisco, California*

In 2017, the CWJC unveiled the *"Comfort Women" Column of Strength* in San Francisco, marking it the first major U.S. city to accept a memorial dedicated to the "comfort women" victims. The statue features three young women—Chinese, Filipina, and Korean—standing together, representing the shared suffering of victims. Below them, a life-sized figure of Hak-sun Kim looks up at them, symbolizing remembrance and resilience (Mirkinson, 2020). The statue's installation and the subsequent acceptance by the city as a city asset led Osaka, Japan, to sever its 60-year-old sister city relationship with San Francisco (McCurry, 2018).

Global Expansion and Challenges

Memorials honoring "comfort women" have emerged worldwide, including in Canada, Australia, Germany, Italy, China, Taiwan, and the Philippines. However, as mentioned in Chapter 3, the Japanese government has actively opposed these efforts, lobbying foreign governments and engaging in legal battles to prevent or remove these statues. At the same time, local communities and international allies continue to stand in solidarity to preserve them.

In the private sector, public controversy also persists, as some denialist groups, scholars, and journalists continue to challenge the historical accuracy of the "comfort women" system, further politicizing the issue. Despite these challenges, "comfort women" memorials continue to be erected worldwide, ensuring that survivors' voices and stories remain integral to global history. These memorials serve as a lasting reminder of past injustices and a call to action to prevent similar human rights violations in the future.

42

Teaching Conflict-Related Sexual Violence Through Human Rights Education:
The Case of the Japanese Military's "Comfort Women"

Lesson Plan: *If Statues Could Talk*

Description
This lesson teaches about the "comfort women" issue through the *Peace Monument* in Glendale, California. Students will analyze the statue and explain how the Japanese right-wing government has been denying the history of "comfort women."

Objectives
By the end of this lesson, students will be able to
- use their observational, inferential, and questioning skills to analyze a "comfort women" statue; and
- explain why the "comfort women" statues are controversial.

NCSS Theme
🔟 CIVIC IDEALS AND PRACTICES

Sources
- Source A: "'It Is Not Coming Down': San Francisco Defends 'Comfort Women' Statue as Japan Protests," by C. Hauser, October 4, 2018, *The New York Times* (**www.nytimes.com/2018/10/04/us/osaka-sf-comfort-women-statue.html**)
- Source B: "Japanese PM Asked German Leader for Help in Removing 'Comfort Women' Statue," Kyodo News, May 11, 2022 (**https://english.kyodonews.net/articles/-/33251**)
- Source C: "German Students Say University Caved to Right-Wing Pressure to Remove 'Comfort Women' Statue," by J. Noh, March 15, 2023, *Hankyoreh* (**https://english.hani.co.kr/arti/english_edition/e_international/1083751.html**)
- See Appendix for images and sample VTS questions.

Lesson Activities (45 minutes)
Opening Discussion (5 minutes)
Last class, we learned about the history of "comfort women." Who were "comfort women"? Wait for students' responses. *That is very good! Today, let's continue learning about the "comfort women" issue through statues.* Project the following two questions on the board in front of the classroom:
1. Have you seen any statues or memorials? If so, what was it?
2. What purpose do statues and memorials serve?

Ask volunteers to share their answers. Tell students that there are numerous statues and memorials in the United States and other countries to memorialize the sufferings of the "comfort women."

Statue Analysis (10 minutes)
1. Project the images of the *Peace Monument* in Glendale, California (Figure 5.1 in the appendix), on the board in front of the classroom. Ask students to look

closely and examine it quietly for a minute or two.

2. Use the Visual Thinking Strategies (VTS) (Grand Valley State University, **www. gvsu.edu/artmuseum/visual-thinking-strategies-152.htm**) to ask probing questions (sample questions are available in the appendix). Consider the following teaching tips:

   a. Avoid praising students' responses, as your praises will likely discourage creative and divergent thinking among students.

   b. Avoid inserting information. Let students look closely and reason out their responses, rather than discussing the facts. If a student comes to a factually incorrect conclusion, gently correct if absolutely necessary during your classroom lesson, not during the VTS conversation. The goal is not to share information but to encourage critical and creative thinking.

Mini-Lecture (5 minutes)

Reveal the symbolic meaning behind the statue's features, as inscribed on the memorial's plaque:

- Torn hair symbolizes the girl being snatched from her home by the Imperial Japanese Army.
- Tight fists represent the girl's firm resolve for a deliverance of justice.
- Bare and unsettled feet represent having been abandoned by the cold and unsympathetic world.
- Bird on the girl's shoulder symbolizes a bond between us and the deceased victims.
- Empty chair symbolizes survivors who are dying of old age without having yet witnessed justice.
- Shadow of the girl is that of an old grandma, symbolizing passage of time spent in silence.
- Butterfly in shadow represents hope that victims may resurrect one day to receive their apology. (Historical Marker Database, 2023)

News Gallery (20 minutes)

1. Divide the class into three groups. Assign each group a news article (see Sources A, B, and C) and ask them to read and discuss the following questions for 10 minutes:

   a. What is the title of the news article?

   b. What does the title tell you?

   c. Who is opposing the statue? Why?

2. Call on each group to share their answers.

Conclusion (5 minutes)

Teachers can end the lesson with these words: *The Japanese government strongly opposes "comfort women" statues around the world and exerts political pressure to have them removed.*

44

Teaching Conflict-Related Sexual Violence Through Human Rights Education:
The Case of the Japanese Military's "Comfort Women"

Officials argue that these young women were not forced into sexual slavery. However, from numerous survivors' testimonies, including the one of Grandma Lee from the last class, we know that many young women and girls were indeed forced into the system of military sexual slavery. How do you view the Japanese government's denial? What actions can you take to help protect these statues? I'd like to know your thoughts through a reflection journal.

Assessments

1. Reflection Journal: Ask students to write a reflection journal, answering the following three questions:
   a. What makes the "comfort women" statues and memorials controversial?
   b. What can you do to help protect these statues and memorials?
   c. What would you like to say to the Japanese government regarding their attitude toward the "comfort women" history?
2. Other assessments options include the following:
   a. Create a Poster: Students will work in small groups and create a poster to raise public awareness of the importance of the "comfort women" statues and memorials. Exhibit the posters in the school gym or a local public library to educate others. They can also create websites and put the digital images of their posters on their website to influence a larger audience.
   b. Write a News Release: Students will work in small groups. Each group will write a news article and send it to the local newspaper. In the news release, they must address the "comfort women" history and why the public needs to protect the "comfort women" statues and memorials.

Accommodations

- If a student has a vision impairment, the teacher can print out the images of the statue and give them to the student before the statue analysis activity.
- If a student prefers to complete the reflection journal in a different format, the teacher should work with the student and choose the best format for that student. Options may include making a video response, recording an audio response, composing a piece of music, or creating visuals like a drawing, painting, infographic, etc.

Extension Activities

There are 15 "comfort women" statues and memorials in the United States. Teachers can choose other statues or memorials and design a lesson by using the Visual Thinking Strategies. If a statue or memorial happens to be close to your school, taking students on a field trip would be ideal. Table 5.1 in this chapter shows the locations of some of the "comfort women" memorials.

Appendix

Supporting Materials for *If Statues Could Talk* Lesson

Figure 5.1 *Peace Monument* or the *Girl Statue*

Note. The *Peace Monument*, Glendale, CA, is the fourth iteration of the *Statue of Peace* in Seoul, South Korea, designed by Kim Seo-kyung and Kim Eun-sung. *Peace monument* [Bronze statue], established by the Korean American Forum of California, 2013, Glendale Central Park, Glendale, California.

VTS Scaffolded Questions

After asking each of the following questions, avoid praising students for their responses. Simply summarize student responses using neutral language. For example, "Maria notices the girl's bare feet." This keeps the conversation open to other interpretations by other students.

1. What is going on in this piece of artwork?
2. What do you see to make you say that?
3. What more can you find?

Afterword

Averting war is the work of politicians; establishing peace is the work of education.

—Maria Montessori

Discussion of sexual violence remains a societal taboo in diverse societies across the globe. Conflict-related sexual violence (CRSV) is generally hidden in public narratives of historical and contemporary warfare. Significantly, such sexual violence is also commonly overlooked both in discussions of reparations to address past and ongoing injustices, and in initiatives to promote peace and reconciliation. Jing Williams and Phyllis Kim are to be congratulated on this initiative, not only in opening a discussion about these sensitive issues among teachers and teacher educators, but also in providing concrete suggestions and lesson plans for social studies teachers on how the subject might be explored, using a human rights education (HRE) pedagogy. The National Council for the Social Studies is also to be congratulated in facilitating this discussion through supporting this publication. Building just peace is a challenging task and much depends on the courage of educators in taking forward the project of justice and peace.

Why Adopt a Human Rights-Based Approach to Conflict-Related Sexual Violence?

The application of human rights principles and a human rights pedagogy to discuss CRSV is important because it provides teachers and students with the security of a normative set of principles and a classroom environment in which complex, yet previously hidden narratives, both historical and contemporary, can be explored openly and respectfully, recognizing that participants bring different experiences and understandings to the subject matter.

The contemporary human rights framework was instigated after World War II as an intended means of enabling justice and peace in the world by codifying international relations through the United Nations (UN) Charter (1945) and presenting a set of guiding principles in the form of the Universal Declaration of Human Rights (UDHR, 1948) for the conduct of nation-states toward each other, setting out their duties toward those living in their territories and providing a set of principles which might enable people to live peaceably together. Importantly, the international human rights framework included, from the start, not just the right to education, but the right to education in human rights. Given the momentum of antidemocratic and authoritarian movements, there has probably never been a time, since the founding of the UN 80 years ago, when global efforts to renew and strengthen education for democracy and human rights have been more important than they are today.

Teachers have a duty under the UDHR and subsequent treaties to teach about and for human rights, justice, and peace in the world. The UDHR (1948) states,

> Education shall be directed to the full development of the human personality and to the strengthening of respect for human rights and fundamental freedoms. It shall promote understanding, tolerance and friendship among all nations, racial

47

Teaching Conflict-Related Sexual Violence Through Human Rights Education:
The Case of the Japanese Military's "Comfort Women"

or religious groups, and shall further the activities of the United Nations for the maintenance of peace. (art. 26, para. 2)

Subsequent binding human rights instruments, notably the UN International Covenant on Economic, Social, and Cultural Rights (1966) and the UN Convention on the Rights of the Child (1989) have confirmed the duty of signatory parties and teachers to provide HRE, outlining what it should address.

The Long-Lasting and Widespread Impact of Conflict-Related Sexual Violence

Margot Wallström, Special Representative of the UN Secretary-General on Sexual Violence in Conflict, highlights how CRSV, whether it is state-initiated and systematic, as in the case explored in this volume, or often more randomly enacted, serves as a means of inflicting fear and exerting power and control on whole communities, *with long-lasting societal effects*. Individuals, communities, and nations cannot heal, and peace cannot be achieved until we understand more fully how CRSV's long-term impact is not only devastating for the lives of individuals and their families but extends to whole societies.

The damage of CRSV impacts all parties, whether they be aggressors, victims of aggression, or apparent bystanders. There are rarely, if ever, innocent bystander nation-states, since under international law, signatory parties have a duty to act to prevent, end, and bring to justice the perpetrators of crimes against humanity. When unlawful actions that cause large-scale suffering or death to civilians occur, other nation-states have a duty to ensure that perpetrators are brought to justice, since under the 1998 Rome Statute, the treaty that set up the International Criminal Court, such suffering is likely to constitute crimes against humanity. Those nation-states that provide aggressors with economic or military support, and those that fail to take a stand when they are presented with evidence of such crimes, are implicated in them.

Teaching Difficult Histories

History education in most, if not all contexts, tends to focus on the history of the nation. All nations, and especially those with past colonial enterprises, have histories which are frequently glossed over in schools. Jing Williams and Phyllis Kim explore the human trafficking and sexual slavery of women in East and Southeast Asia that took place under the auspices of the Imperial Japanese Army in the first half of the 20th century, practices that were subsequently perpetuated by other authorities after World War II. Processes of denial and revisionism followed for many decades, and it took considerable courage for victims to come forward and tell their stories. When teaching about human trafficking, sexual slavery, denial, and revisionism as elements of CRSV, teachers are also addressing horrors that continue to be perpetuated today. In facing history, social studies teachers are also facing contemporary problems and contemporary human rights abuses. They are effectively supporting students in distinguishing truth from falsehood in contemporary politics, confronting some of the key threats to democracy, and preparing students to engage actively as citizens. In increasingly authoritarian contexts, such work demands courage. The tools and resources which Williams and Kim provide, along with the mnemonic device of the UN Declaration on Human Rights Education and Training (2011) of education *about*, *through*, and *for* human rights, support this courageous work.

48

Teaching Conflict-Related Sexual Violence Through Human Rights Education:
The Case of the Japanese Military's "Comfort Women"

Teaching With Narratives

In many educational contexts, and especially in the context of history education and history textbooks, women's narratives remain marginalized or absent (Osler, 1994; Parveen et al., 2025). This volume, in addressing CRSV, centers women's narratives and women's testimonies, and in doing so, reasserts both the role that narratives can play in HRE (especially in bringing it closer to the everyday lives of students) and the contributions that women have made to the overall human rights project of justice and peace in the world (Adami, 2021; Osler, 2015; Osler & Zhu, 2011). The very women who have been the victims of CRSV are also those who have rejected victimhood and have engaged in a struggle for justice, building international cooperation and solidarity, and campaigning for justice and recognition. The women highlighted here are powerful advocates for the rights of the vulnerable.

A Way Forward for Human Rights Education

This contribution to HRE by Jing Williams and Phyllis Kim could not be timelier. "Establishing peace is the work of education," as Maria Montessori noted, and it is an urgent, challenging, and courageous task.

The UN structures and the human rights framework is imperfect, but they are the best we have. We live in a turbulent and troubled world where education for human rights and social justice is needed as much as it has ever been. Human rights and human rights education offer ways forward for having a dialogue across differences and finding peaceable solutions to problems. Teachers and students can find ways to discuss difficult and sensitive topics in history and across the social studies curriculum that might otherwise be avoided.

Williams and Kim set out why CRSV needs to be discussed as part of the wider project of working toward justice and peace in the world. They argue convincingly that CRSV needs to be part of our narratives of historical and contemporary conflicts, narratives in which women, generally the primary victims of CRSV, have long been marginalized. Until we find ways of talking about sexual violence, and especially sexual violence carried out as a weapon of war, we cannot hope to find lasting ways to end conflicts, achieve just peace, or promote long-term justice and reconciliation. This volume offers teachers many starting points for engaging in this important work.

Audrey Osler is Professor Emerita of Citizenship and Human Rights Education at the University of Leeds, founding editor of *Human Rights Education Review*, Chair of International Association for Human Rights Education, and a prize-winning author. She is internationally recognized for her work on child rights and education for reconciliation in conflict-ridden settings and has taught in universities across the globe. Her books are translated into Chinese, Japanese, Korean, and Persian. Her most personal, *Where Are You From? No, Where Are You Really From?* (Virago, 2023), uses family narratives to discuss colonialism, migration, and belonging. In 2025, her monograph *Human Rights and Schooling: An Ethical Framework for Teaching for Social Justice* was selected as an excellent book by the National Academy of Sciences, Republic of Korea.

She can be reached via email at **a.h.osler@leeds.ac.uk**.

49

Teaching Conflict-Related Sexual Violence Through Human Rights Education:
The Case of the Japanese Military's "Comfort Women"

References

Adami, R. (2021). Revisiting the past: human rights education and epistemic justice. *Human Rights Education Review, 4* (3), 5–23. **https://doi.org/10.7577/hrer.4486**

The Charter of the United Nations and Statute of the International Court of Justice, June 26, 1945, **www.un.org/en/about-us/universal-declaration-of-human-rights**

Osler, A. (1994). Still hidden from history? The representation of women in recently published history textbooks. *Oxford Review of Education, 20* (2), 219–235. **https://doi.org/10.1080/0305498940200206**

Osler, A. (2015). The stories we tell: Exploring narrative in education for justice and equality in multicultural contexts. *Multicultural Education Review, 7* (1–2), 12–25. **https://doi.org/10.1080/2005615X.2015.1048605**

Osler, A., & Zhu, J. (2011) Narratives in teaching and research for justice and human rights. *Education, Citizenship and Social Justice, 6* (3), 223–235. **https://doi.org/10.1177/1746197911417414**

Parveen, N., Rodrigues, G., Zainulabidin, N., & Ashraf, D. (2025). Human rights education in primary school textbooks: insights from Pakistan. *Human Rights Education Review, 8* (2), 296–308. **https://doi.org/10.1080/25355406.2025.2536849**

United Nations Convention on the Rights of the Child, November 20, 1989, **www.ohchr.org/en/instruments-mechanisms/instruments/convention-rights-child**

United Nations Declaration on Human Rights Education and Training, December 19, 2011, **www.ohchr.org/en/resources/educators/human-rights-education-training/11-united-nations-declaration-human-rights-education-and-training-2011**

United Nations International Covenant on Economic, Social and Cultural Rights, December 16, 1966, **www.ohchr.org/en/instruments-mechanisms/instruments/international-covenant-economic-social-and-cultural-rights**

United Nations Rome Statute of the International Criminal Court, July 17, 1998, **https://ihl-databases.icrc.org/en/ihl-treaties/icc-statute-1998**

United Nations Universal Declaration of Human Rights, December 10, 1948, **www.un.org/en/about-us/universal-declaration-of-human-rights**

50

Teaching Conflict-Related Sexual Violence Through Human Rights Education:
The Case of the Japanese Military's "Comfort Women"

Further Resources on "Comfort Women" Education

Resources in bold are recommended starting points for foundational understanding. We encourage readers to explore all resources, as each contributes meaningfully to the topic.

Websites and Online Resources

Asia-Pacific Journal: Japan Focus, Fact Sheet on Japanese Military "Comfort Women," **https://apjjf.org/asia-pacific-journal-feature/4829/article**

Bisland, B. M., Kim, J., & Shin, S. (2019). Teaching about the comfort women during World War II and the use of personal stories of the victims. *Education About Asia, 24*(3), 58–63. **www.asianstudies.org/publications/eaa/archives/teaching-about-the-comfort-women-during-world-war-ii-and-the-use-of-personal-stories-of-the-victims**

Comfort Women Action for Redress & Education (CARE, formerly known as KAFC), **https://comfortwomenaction.org**

"Comfort Women" Justice Coalition, **https://remembercomfortwomen.org**

Comfort Women Resource Center, UCLA, **www.international.ucla.edu/cks/care**

International Committee for Joint Nomination of Documents on the Japanese Military "Comfort Women" to UNESCO Memory of the World Register, **http://voicecw.org**

JUJU Project: **https://juju-project.net/en**

Women's Active Museum on War and Peace, **https://wam-peace.org/en**

Lesson Plans

Bisland, B. M., Kim, J., & Shin, S. (2019). Teaching about the comfort women during World War II and the use of personal stories of the victims. *Education About Asia, 24*(3), 58–63. **www.asianstudies.org/wp-content/uploads/teaching-about-the-comfort-women-during-world-war-ii-and-the-use-of-personal-stories-of-the-victims.pdf**

Comfort Women Action for Redress and Education (CARE), **https://comfortwomeneducation.org**

Education for Social Justice Foundation, **www.e4sjf.org/8203remembering-and-honoring-comfort-women.html**

Kindschi, L. A. (n.d.). *Comfort Women—Teaching to the Truth.* Korea Society, **www.koreasociety.org/images/pdf/KoreanStudies/Curriculum_Materials/LessonbyTime/4_Modern/Comfort_Women__Teaching_to_the_Truth.pdf**

Riddell, A. (n.d.). *Comfort Women during World War II.* National Women's History Museum: **www.womenshistory.org/resources/lesson-plan/comfort-women-during-world-war-ii**

Williams, J. A., & Cha, B. (2023). "Comfort women:" The contention of historical narratives. *Oregon Journal of the Social Studies, 11*(2), 96–116. **www.researchgate.net/publication/376646352_Comfort_Women_The_Contention_of_Historical_Narratives**

Documentaries and Films

The Apology (2016), directed by Tiffany Hsiung; 104 minutes. This documentary follows three former "comfort women," who retell their shameful past. (Available on Amazon Prime and Vimeo)

51

Teaching Conflict-Related Sexual Violence Through Human Rights Education:
The Case of the Japanese Military's "Comfort Women"

Fifty Years of Silence (1994), directed by Ned Lander; 57 minutes. This is the life story of Jan Ruff-O'Herne, a Dutch girl who was forced to be a "comfort woman" when she was 21 years old. (Available on Kanopy for free with a participating public library card or participating college or university login)

Gai Shanxi and Her Sisters (2007), directed by Zhongyi Ban; 80 minutes. This documentary tells the story of one Chinese woman's ordeal as a "comfort woman" for the Japanese Army during World War II. (Available free on YouTube with English subtitles)

Herstory (2018), directed by Kyu-dong Min; 121 minutes. This feature film is about a businesswoman and the Korean "comfort women" survivors who took on the Japanese government in a trial seeking reparations and a formal apology. (Available on Amazon Prime)

Ianfu (2018), directed by Sophie Emma Wells; 10 minutes. This film is based on accounts from Hwang Keum-ju. (Available free on YouTube)

In the Name of the Emperor (1995), directed by Nancy Tong, 52 minutes, "Comfort Women" portion edited by the director (4:26). (Available free on YouTube with English subtitles.)

Shusenjo: The Main Battleground of the Comfort Women Issue (2018), directed by Miki Dezaki; 121 minutes. This documentary presents narratives (by deniers) and counternarratives (by supporters and historians) of the "comfort women" issue. (Available free on Kanopy with a participating public library card or participating college or university login; or available on YouTube, Apple TV, and Google Play with a payment)

Silence Broken (1999), directed by Dai Sil Kim-Gibson; 56 minutes. This documentary dramatically combines the testimony of former "comfort women," along with contravening interviews of Japanese soldiers, recruiters, and contemporary scholars who deny the existence of "comfort women" or claim that these victims "did this for money." (Available free on Kanopy with a participating public library card or participating college or university login)

Spirits' Homecoming (2016), directed by Jung-lae Jo; 127 minutes. This feature film is about two girls who are kidnapped by the Japanese Army and taken to a "comfort station" in China. (Available on Amazon Prime)

Twenty Two (2015), directed by Ke Guo; 112 minutes. Twenty-two surviving Chinese comfort women tell their wartime experience. (Available free on YouTube)

Short Videos and Animations

The Comfort Women (HISS, 2016), 5 minutes. This animation is produced with the actual voice of "comfort women" victims. (Available on YouTube with English subtitles, **www.youtube.com/watch?v=ZdEqOdmK62E**)

"Herstory" Story of Seo-woon Chung (2011), directed by Jun-ki Kim; 11 minutes. This animation is produced with the actual voice of Grandma Seo-woon Chung. (Available at UCLA Comfort Women Resource Center, **https://international.ucla.edu/cks/care/comfortwomen_speakup/267550**)

Life as a "Comfort Woman": Story of Kim Bok-dong (2018), by Asian Boss; 18:15. (Available on YouTube, **https://youtu.be/qsT97ax_Xb0?si=d2AeDlv1qq_n-Tuq**)

Never Ending Story (2014), produced by M-LINE STUDIO; 15 minutes. This animation is about the stories of Japanese sex slavery victims. (Available on YouTube with English subtitles, **www.youtube.com/watch?v=Bp8A9TJ48RQ**)

On the controversial 2015 Japan–South Korea Agreement (2016), by CUNY's Asian American Life; 8:17. Part 2. (Available at UCLA online archive, **https://international.ucla.edu/cks/care/comfortwomen_speakup/251234**)

52

Teaching Conflict-Related Sexual Violence Through Human Rights Education:
The Case of the Japanese Military's "Comfort Women"

"Stories Untold" (2017), directed by Jun-ki Kim; 14:29. This animation is produced with the actual voices of the former Japanese soldiers. (Available at UCLA online archive, **https://international.ucla.edu/cks/care/ comfortwomen_speakup/267642**)

Wartime Sex Slaves Fight for Justice in Japan, by "Unreported World" documentary team of British TV Channel 4, 24:03 (Available on YouTube, **https://youtu.be/BZyYyXKG51s?si=jCVM6IJ4Tn_l3IJD**)

Books for Young Adults (English version)
Gendry-Kim, K. S. (2019). *Grass* (J. Hong, Trans.). Drawn and Quarterly.

Han, S.-W. (2023). *Grandmothers, Our Grandmothers: Remembering the "comfort women" of World War II*. Tuttle Publishing.

Moon, Y.-S. (2019). *Trampled Blossoms* (David Carruth, Trans.). Seoul Selection.

Park, J. J. (2015). *Her Tears: A Story about a Comfort Women Halmeoni*. Button Books. **https:// justiceforcomfortwomen.org/wp-content/uploads/2015/10/ec868ceb8580ec9d98eb8888ebacbcec9881 ebacb8-eca080ec9aa9eb9f89-1.pdf**

Yoon, E. J. (2018). *A Cruelty Special to Our Species: Poems*. Ecco.

Yoon, J. (2015). *Balsamina: Touch-Me-Not* (H. Lee, Trans.). Ministry of Gender Equality & Family and Women's Human Rights Commission of Korea.

Books/Chapters for Teachers and Researchers (English Version)
Choi, C., & Yang, H. (2023). *Voices of the Korean comfort women: History rewritten from memories*. Routledge.

Friedman, S. J. (2015). *Silence no more: Voices of comfort women*.

Henson, M. R. (1999). *Comfort woman: A Filipina's story of prostitution and slavery under the Japanese military*. Rowman & Littlefield Publishers.

Hicks, G. (1994). *Comfort women: Japan's brutal regime of enforced prostitution in the second world war*. W. W. Norton & Company.

Jacob, F. (Ed.) (2020). *Stories that make history: The experience and memories of the Japanese military comfort girls-women: Vol. 3. Genocide and mass violence in the age of extremes* (A. Son, Trans.). De Gruyter.

Kim-Gibson, D. S. (1999). *Silence broken: Korean comfort women*. Mid-Prairie Books.

Kim, J. D., Sung, C., & Lee, M. S. (Eds.). (2019). *Comfort women: New perspectives*. Blurb Publisher.

Lee, J.-S., & Halpin, D. P. (Eds.). (2020). *Comfort women: A movement for justice and women's rights in the United States*. Hollym.

Min, P. G., Chung, T., Yim, S. S. (Eds.). (2020). *The transnational movement for the victims of Japanese military sexual slavery: The transnational redress movement for the victims*. De Gruyter Oldenbourg.

Nishino, R., Kim, P., & Onozawa, A. (2018). *Denying the comfort women: The Japanese state's assault on historical truth*. Routledge.

Norma, C. (2017). *The Japanese comfort women and sexual slavery during the China and Pacific Wars*. Bloomsbury.

Qiu, P. (2013). ***Chinese comfort women: Testimonies from imperial Japan's sex slaves***. Oxford University Press.

Teaching Conflict-Related Sexual Violence Through Human Rights Education: The Case of the Japanese Military's "Comfort Women"

Ruff-O'Herne, J. (2008). *Fifty years of silence: The extraordinary memoir of a war rape survivor*. Random House Australia.

Shin, S., Bisland, B. M., & Kim, J. (2021). The violation of human rights during wartime: Teaching about the "comfort women" of World War II and their search for justice. In R. W. Evans (Ed.), *Handbook on teaching social issues*. Information Age Publishing.

Soh, C. S. (2009). *The comfort women: Sexual violence and postcolonial memorial in Korea and Japan*. University of Chicago Press.

Stetz, M. D., & Oh, B. B. C. (2001). **Legacies of the comfort women of World War II**. Routledge.

Tanaka, Y. (2002). *Japan's comfort women: Sexual slavery and prostitution during World War II and the US occupation*. Routledge.

Yoshimi, Y. (2005). **Comfort women: Sexual slavery in the Japanese military during World War II**. Columbia University Press.

Reports, Resolutions, and Government Documents

Dolgopol, U., & Paranjape, S. (1994). *Comfort Women: An Unfinished Ordeal. Report of a Mission*. International Commission of Jurists. **www.icj.org/resource/comfort-women-an-unfinished-ordeal-report-of-a-mission**

H.R. Res. 121, 110th Cong. (2007–2008). **www.congress.gov/bill/110th-congress/house-resolution/121** A resolution expressing the sense of the House of Representatives that the Government of Japan should formally acknowledge, apologize, and accept historical responsibility in a clear and unequivocal manner for its Imperial Armed Forces' coercion of young women into sexual slavery, known to the world as "comfort women," during its colonial and wartime occupation of Asia and the Pacific Islands from the 1930s through the duration of World War II. (2007, July 30).

Kono, Y. (1993, August 4). Statement by the Chief Cabinet Secretary. **www.mofa.go.jp/a_o/rp/ page25e_000343.html**

54

Teaching Conflict-Related Sexual Violence Through Human Rights Education:
The Case of the Japanese Military's "Comfort Women"

References

AGBU Video. (2021, April 23). *Israel Charny: Denial as hate speech* [Video]. YouTube. **www.youtube.com/ watch?v=eoHvVcewd0I**

Akira, F. (2008). The Nanjing atrocity: An interpretive overview. In B. T. Wakabayashi (Ed.), *The Nanjing atrocity, 1937–1938: Complicating the picture* (pp. 29–54). Berghahn Books.

Amnesty International. (2011, March 26). *Sudan: Darfur: Rape as a weapon of war: Sexual violence and its consequences.* **www.amnestyusa.org/reports/sudan-darfur-rape-as-a-weapon-of-war-sexual-violence-and-its-consequences**

Amnesty International. (2017, July 23). *South Sudan: "Do not remain silent": Survivors of sexual violence in South Sudan call for justice and reparations.* **www.amnesty.org/en/documents/afr65/6469/2017/en**

Anonymous. (2005). *A woman in Berlin: Eight weeks in the conquered city: A diary* (P. Boehm, Trans.). Picador.

Argibay, C. M. (2003). Sexual slavery and the "comfort women" of World War II. *Berkeley Journal of International Law, 21*(2), 375–389.

Arirang News. (2022, January 19). *Weekly "Wednesday demonstration" held peacefully, no clashes with far-right groups* [Video]. YouTube. **www.youtube.com/watch?v=Lctm6kqsQjk**

Arumugham, A., & Ying, L. J. (2024, January 19). *Tokyo Women's Tribunal—Voices of the women working behind the scenes (part one).* The Second World War in Asia: Justice Efforts, War Memory, and Reparations Symposium. **https://cil.nus.edu.sg/blogs/tokyo-womens-tribunal-voices-of-the-women-working-behind-the-scenes-part-one/**

Association des Veuves du Génocide (n.d.). *Our story: From tragedy to triumph.* **https://avega-agahozo.org/ about-us/#story**

Baaz, M. E., & Stern, M. (2013). *Sexual violence as a weapon of war? Perceptions, prescriptions, problems in the Congo and beyond.* Zed Books.

Barsocchini, R. J. (2017, October 3). *American rape of Vietnamese women was considered "standard operating procedure."* Counter Punch. **www.counterpunch.org/2017/10/03/american-rape-of-vietnamese-women-was-considered-standard-operating-procedure**

Barstow, A. L. (Ed.). (2000). *War's dirty secret: Rape, prostitution, and other crimes against women.* Pilgrim Press.

Barton, K. C. (2019). What should we teach about human rights? Implications of international research. *Social Education, 83*(4), 212–216.

Barton, K. C., & Levstik, L. S. (2004). *Teaching history for the common good.* Routledge.

Bedrossian, K. (2021, April 24). *The Armenian genocide and acts of denial.* Human Rights Pulse. **www. humanrightspulse.com/mastercontentblog/the-armenian-genocide-and-acts-of-denial**

Bemma, A. (2017, September 8). *South Korea: World's longest protest over comfort women.* Al Jazeera Media Network. **www.aljazeera.com/news/2017/9/8/south-korea-worlds-longest-protest-over-comfort-women?**

55

*Teaching Conflict-Related Sexual Violence Through Human Rights Education:
The Case of the Japanese Military's "Comfort Women"*

The Berliner. (2024, May 24). *Is Berlin planning to remove a statue to Korean "comfort women"?* **www.the-berliner. com/english-news-berlin/statue-of-peace-friedenstatue-kai-wegner-plan-remove-statue-korean-comfort-women**

Binkley, C. (2021, March 8). *Harvard professor ignites uproar over "comfort women" claims.* AP News. **https:// apnews.com/article/j-mark-ramseyer-harvard-paper-comfort-women-dbebb62b01045c23036089ca341 5de64**

Bisland, B. M., Kim, J., & Shin, S. (2019). Teaching about the comfort women during World War II and the use of personal stories of the victims. *Education About Asia, 24*(3): 58–63. **www.asianstudies.org/publications/eaa/ archives/teaching-about-the-comfort-women-during-world-war-ii-and-the-use-of-personal-stories-of-the-victims**

Blakemore, E. (2025, May 28). *The brutal history of Japan's "comfort women."* History. **www.history.com/news/ comfort-women-japan-military-brothels-korea**

Brander, P., De Witte, L., Ghanea, N., Gomes, R., Keen, E., Nikitina, A., & Pinkeviciute, J. (2023). *COMPASS: Manual for human rights education with young people* (2nd ed.). Council of Europe. **https://rm.coe.int/compass-2023-eng-final-web/1680af992c**

Brownmiller, S. (1975). *Against our will: Men, women and rape.* Fawcett Books.

CBS News. (2021, April 26). *Turkey's president slams Biden's acknowledgement of Armenian genocide* [Video]. YouTube. **www.youtube.com/watch?v=1SyNdkEg48k**

Cha, B., & Williams, J. (2025). Empowering global citizens: Teaching the "comfort women" history through human rights education in South Korea. *Human Rights Education Review,* 1–15. **https://doi.org/10.1080/2535 5406.2025.2555995**

Chang, I. (1997). *The rape of Nanking: The forgotten Holocaust of World War II.* Penguin Books.

Charny, I. W. (2001). The psychological satisfaction of denials of the Holocaust or other genocides by non-extremists or bigots, and even by known scholars. *IDEA: A Journal of Social Issues, 6*(1). **www.researchgate. net/publication/297503028_The_psychological_satisfaction_of_denials_of_the_Holocaust_or_other_ genocides_by_non-extremists_or_bigots_and_even_by_known_scholars**

Charny, I. W. (2003). A classification of denials of the Holocaust and other genocides. *Journal of Genocide Research, 5*(1), 11–34.

Cho, K. (2017, November 1). UNESCO postpones registration of comfort women archival materials due to pressure from Japanese government. *Hankyoreh.* **https://english.hani.co.kr/arti/english_edition/e_ international/817040.html**

Cho, K. (2022, May 12). Japanese PM asked German chancellor to take down "comfort women" statue in Berlin. *Hankyoreh.* **https://english.hani.co.kr/arti/english_edition/e_international/1042632.html**

Choe, S.-H. (2023, May 2). A brutal sex trade built for American soldiers. *The New York Times.* **www.nytimes. com/2023/05/02/world/asia/korea-us-comfort-women-sexual-slavery.html**

Choi, B., & Park, J. (2024, January 25). Glendale city council candidates promise to protect comfort women statue. *The Korean Daily.* **www.koreadailyus.com/glendale-city-council-candidates-promise-to-protect-comfort-women-statue**

Choi, C., & Yang, H. (Eds. & Trans.). (2023). *Voices of the Korean comfort women: History rewritten from memories.*

56

Teaching Conflict-Related Sexual Violence Through Human Rights Education: The Case of the Japanese Military's "Comfort Women"

Routledge.

Comfort Women Action for Redress and Education. (2025, September 1). *SF library exhibition: "Comfort women" opens on Sept 26, 2025!!* https://comfortwomenaction.org/2025/09/01/sf-library-exhibition-comfort-women-opens-on-sept-26-2025

"Comfort Women" Justice Coalition. (2021, May 6). *San Francisco supervisors pass resolution in support of "comfort women."* https://remembercomfortwomen.org/comfort-women-justice-victory/

Comfort Women Resource Center. (n.d.). *TS-18. Jan Ruff O'Herne, an Australian survivor from Dutch East Indies.* www.international.ucla.edu/cks/care/comfortwomen_speakup/267664

Constante, A. (2017a, March 31). *Supreme Court declines case over lawsuit to remove "comfort women" memorial.* NBC News. www.nbcnews.com/news/asian-america/supreme-court-declines-case-over-lawsuit-remove-comfort-women-memorial-n740996

Constante, A. (2017b, December 5). *Osaka mayor says he will end San Francisco sister city ties over "comfort women" statue.* NBC News. www.nbcnews.com/news/asian-america/osaka-mayor-says-he-will-end-san-francisco-sister-city-n826656

Dahl, R. (2015, March 21). Comfort whitewash [Political cartoon]. *The Japan Times.*

The Dinah Project. (2025). *A quest for justice: October 7 and beyond.* https://thedinahproject.org

Dovhan, I., & Hyun, S. S. (2025, June 11). *"Stop using women's bodies as battlefields!" Interview with Iryna Dovhan, advocate for victims of sexual violence in the Ukraine War and member of the global network SEMA.* Research Institute on Japanese Military Sexual Slavery. https://kyeol.kr/en/node/579

Dudden, A. (2021, March 1). Supplement to special issue: Academic integrity at stake: The Ramseyer article—Four letters. *Asia-Pacific Journal: Japan Focus, 19*(5). https://apjjf.org/2021/5/ToC2

European Parliament. (2007, December 13). *European Parliament resolution of 13 December 2007 on justice for the "comfort women" (sex slaves in Asia before and during World War II).* www.europarl.europa.eu/doceo/document/TA-6-2007-0632_EN.html

European Union. (2018, April 26). *Council decision (CFSP) 2018/655 of 26 April 2018 amending decision 2013/184/CFSP concerning restrictive measures against Myanmar/Burma.* https://eur-lex.europa.eu/eli/dec/2018/655/oj/eng

Expression of concern: "Contracting for sex in the Pacific War" [International Review of Law and Economics, Volume 65, March 2021, 105971]. (2021). *International Review of Law and Economics, 65,* Article 105985. https://doi.org/10.1016/j.irle.2021.105985

Fangrad, A. (2013). *Wartime rape and sexual violence: An examination of the perpetrators, motivations, and functions of sexual violence against Jewish women during the Holocaust.* AuthorHouse.

Fifield, A. (2015, February 9). U.S. academics condemn Japanese efforts to revise history of "comfort women." *The Washington Post.* www.washingtonpost.com/world/asia_pacific/american-academics-condemn-japanese-efforts-to-revise-history-of-comfort-women/2015/02/09/e795fc1c-38f0-408f-954a-7f989779770a_story.html

Flowers, N. (2000). *The human rights education handbook: Effective practices for learning, action, and change.* The Human Rights Resource Center; Stanley Foundation. http://hrlibrary.umn.edu/edumat/pdf/hreh.pdf

57

Teaching Conflict-Related Sexual Violence Through Human Rights Education:
The Case of the Japanese Military's "Comfort Women"

Frymark, K. (2015, May 20). *Germany supports the quota scheme for refugees in the EU*. Center for Eastern Studies. **www.osw.waw.pl/en/publikacje/analyses/2015–05–20/germany-supports-quota-scheme-refugees-eu**

Gebhardt, M. (2017). *Crimes unspoken: The rape of German women at the end of the second world war* (N. Somers, Trans.). Polity. (Original work published 2015)

Gersen, J. S. (2021, February 25). Seeking the true story of the comfort women. *The New Yorker*. **www.newyorker.com/culture/annals-of-inquiry/seeking-the-true-story-of-the-comfort-women-j-mark-ramseyer**

Global Sanctions. (n.d.). *Burma/Myanmar*. **https://globalsanctions.com/region/burma/**

Government of Canada. (2017, February 21). *Canada to welcome 1200 Yazidi and other survivors of Daesh* [News release]. **www.canada.ca/en/immigration-refugees-citizenship/news/2017/02/canada_to_welcome1200yazidiandothersurvivorsofdaesh.html**

Griffin, J. (2019, January 19). *Women raped by Korean soldiers during Vietnam War still awaiting apology. The Guardian*. **www.theguardian.com/global-development/2019/jan/19/women-raped-by-korean-soldiers-during-vietnam-war-still-awaiting-apology**

Grossmann, A. (1995). A question of silence: The rape of German women by occupation soldiers. *MIT Press, 72*, 42–63.

Gruhl, W. (2010). *Imperial Japan's World War Two, 1931–1945*. Transaction Publishers.

Hall, A. (2010, February 28). *German woman breaks silence about Red Army rapes*. The Telegraph. **www.telegraph.co.uk/news/worldnews/europe/germany/7338034/German-woman-breaks-silence-about-Red-Army-rapes.html**

Hauser, C. (2018, October 4). "It is not coming down": San Francisco defends "comfort women" statue as Japan protests. *The New York Times*. **www.nytimes.com/2018/10/04/us/osaka-sf-comfort-women-statue.html**

Hedgepeth, S. M., & Saidel, R. G. (Eds.). (2010). *Sexual violence against Jewish women during the Holocaust*. Brandeis University Press.

Henry, N. (2011). *War and rape: Law, memory and justice*. Routledge.

Hicks, G. (1994). *Comfort women: Japan's brutal regime of enforced prostitution in the Second World War*. W. W. Norton.

Historical Marker Database. (2023, January 30). *Korean comfort women statue: Peace monument*. **www.hmdb.org/m.asp?m=138945**

Hosaka, Y. (2021, November 18). *Why did the 2015 Japan-Korea "comfort women" agreement fall apart?* The Diplomat. **https://thediplomat.com/2021/11/why-did-the-2015-japan-korea-comfort-women-agreement-fall-apart**

Howard, C. (2023, March 22). *The Heroinat Memorial in Pristina, Kosovo*. **https://cherylhoward.com/heroinat-memorial**

H.R. Res. 121, 110 Cong. (2007). **www.congress.gov/bill/110th-congress/house-resolution/121/text**

Hu, E. (2017, November 13). *"Comfort women" memorial statues, a thorn in Japan's side, now sit on Korean buses*. NPR. **www.npr.org/sections/parallels/2017/11/13/563838610/comfort-woman-memorial-statues-a-**

58

Teaching Conflict-Related Sexual Violence Through Human Rights Education:
The Case of the Japanese Military's "Comfort Women"

thorn-in-japans-side-now-sit-on-korean-buses

Human Rights Council. (2024, March 18). *Report of the independent international commission of inquiry on Ukraine.* www.ohchr.org/sites/default/files/documents/hrbodies/hrcouncil/coiukraine/a-hrc-55–66-aev.pdf

Human Rights Watch. (2016, April 5). *Iraq: Women suffer under ISIS.* www.hrw.org/news/2016/04/06/iraq-women-suffer-under-isis

International Committee of the Red Cross. (1929). *Geneva Convention Relative to the Treatment of Prisoners of War* (Article 3). https://ihl-databases.icrc.org/en/ihl-treaties/gc-pow-1929/article-3?activeTab=

International Symposium on Sexual Violence in Conflict and Beyond. (2006, June 21–23). *Report on the international symposium on sexual violence in conflict and beyond.* https://documentation.lastradainternational.org/lsidocs/unfpa_report_sexual_violence_070402.pdf

Ito, S. (2017). *Black box.* The Feminist Press.

Jacob, F. (Ed.) (2020). *Stories that make history: The experience and memories of the Japanese military comfort girls-women: Vol. 3. Genocide and mass violence in the age of extremes* (A. Son, Trans.). De Gruyter.

Jang, P. (2021, July 15). Wednesday demonstration for "comfort women" victims hit 1,500 mark. *Hankyoreh.* https://english.hani.co.kr/arti/english_edition/e_national/1003715.html

Janoski, S. (2025, February 20). Ukrainian female POWs detail horrors of Russian captivity, including torture and rape: "Threat of death was always there." *New York Post.* https://nypost.com/2025/02/20/world-news/captured-ukrainian-women-detail-horrors-of-russian-captivity

Jung, M. (2019, January 5). "Comfort woman" statue removed in Philippines. *The Korea Times.* www.koreatimes.co.kr/www/nation/2019/01/120_261460.html

Kang, H. M. (2018, November 27). South Korea decides to dismantle "comfort women" reconciliation and healing foundation. *The Diplomat.* https://thediplomat.com/2018/11/south-korea-decides-to-dismantle-comfort-women-reconciliation-and-healing-foundation

Kim, G. (2011). Hankook jeonjaengwa hankookkun wianbu moonjaerul dorabonda [Looking back at the Korean War and the Korean military comfort women issue]. *Goosulsa Yeongu, 2*(1), 117–140.

Kim, H. (2012). Teaching about the Korean comfort women. *Social Education, 76*(5), 251–252.

Kim, I. (2024, August 4). *My sisters in the stars—The story of Lee Yong-soo* [Video]. YouTube. www.youtube.com/watch?v=GkPclUSl1ml

Kim, M. (2024, September 16). How a memorial to WWII sex slaves ignited a battle in Berlin. *Los Angeles Times.* www.latimes.com/world-nation/story/2024–09–16/japans-campaign-against-memorials-to-comfort-women-comes-to-an-unlikely-place

Kim, P. (2020). Looking back at 10 years of the "comfort women" movement in the U.S. In P. G. Min, T. R. Chung, & S. S. Yim (Eds.), *The transnational redress movement for the victims of Japanese military sexual slavery* (pp. 179–200). De Gruyter Oldenbourg.

Kim, S. (2021, March 31). Japanese textbooks don't acknowledge "comfort women" system's coercive nature. *Hankyoreh.* https://english.hani.co.kr/arti/english_edition/e_international/989040.html

Kim-Gibson, D. S. (1999). *Silence broken: Korean comfort women.* Mid-Prairie Books.

59

Teaching Conflict-Related Sexual Violence Through Human Rights Education:
The Case of the Japanese Military's "Comfort Women"

Köpp, G. (2010). *Warum war ich bloß ein Mädchen?: Das Trauma einer Flucht 1945* [Why did I have to be a girl?: The trauma of a 1945 escape]. F. A. Herbig Verlag.

Korean American Forum of California. (2013). *Peace monument* [Bronze statue]. Glendale Central Park, Glendale, California.

The Korean Council for Justice and Remembrance. (n.d.). *The world's longest protest: Wednesday Demonstration, held every Wednesday at 12pm.* **www.archivecenter.net/wednesdaydemo/archive/ArchiveIntro.do**

KYEOL. (2025, February 24). *Exploring the "Women's International War Crimes Tribunal on the Trial of Japan's Military Sexual Slavery in 2000" through the archives.* **https://kyeol.kr/en/node/243**

Kyodo News. (2022, May 11). *Japanese PM asked German leader for help in removing "comfort women" statue.* **https://english.kyodonews.net/articles/-/33251**

Lamb, C. (2020). *Our bodies, their battlefield: What war does to women.* William Collins.

Landorf, H. (2009). Toward a philosophy of global education. In T. F. Kirkwood-Tucker (Ed.), *Visions in global education: The globalization of curriculum and pedagogy in teacher education and schools: Perspectives from Canada, Russia, and the United States* (pp. 47–67). Peter Lang.

Lawlor, R. (2022). The Stuttgart incident: Sexual violence and the uses of history. *Diplomatic History, 46*(1), 70–96. **https://doi.org/10.1093/dh/dhab084**.

Lee, J. (2022, August 17). 30 years of "comfort women" rallies mark world's longest peace protest. *Hankyoreh.* **https://english.hani.co.kr/arti/english_edition/e_national/1026300.html**

Lee, N.-Y. (2018). Un/forgettable histories of US camptown prostitution in South Korea: Women's experiences of sexual labor and government policies. *Sexualities, 21*(5–6), 751–775. **https://doi.org/10.1177/1363460716688683**

MakingHistories. (2024, February 28). *"Comfort women" Wednesday demonstrations: Memory practices and troubled pasts* [Video]. YouTube. **www.youtube.com/ watch?v=fYjwPDiu8rQ**

Makumeno, E. (2025, February 16). *Second DR Congo city falls to Rwanda-backed rebels.* BBC. **www.bbc.com/news/articles/c0rqr8q5v52o?vcrmeid=wut3r1maT0WOkKYK107YvA&vcrmiid=LqjwXyNNkk6Bqb_Jc9c-Gg**

Manahan, J. (2018, May 10). *Sculptor cried over removal of "comfort woman" statue.* ABS-CBN News. **www.abs-cbn.com/focus/05/10/18/sculptor-cried-over-removal-of-comfort-woman-statue**

Martin, A. (2015, January 15). U.S. publisher rebuffs Japan on "comfort women" revision. *The Wall Street Journal.* **www.wsj.com/articles/u-s-publisher-rejects-japan-over-textbook-on-comfort-women-1421299438**

McCurry, J. (2015, January 15). *Japan urges US publisher to remove comfort women from textbooks.* The Guardian. **www.theguardian.com/world/2015/jan/15/japan-urges-us-publisher-delete-references-comfort-women**

McCurry, J. (2018, October 4). *Osaka drops San Francisco as sister city over "comfort women" statue.* The Guardian. **www.theguardian.com/world/2018/oct/04/osaka-drops-san-francisco-as-sister-city-over-comfort-women-statue**

Memorial Hall of the Victims in Nanjing Massacre by Japanese Invaders. (n.d.). *Introduction to the site of Nanjing Lijixiang comfort station.* **https://www.19371213.com.cn/en/lijixiang/introduction/**

60

Teaching Conflict-Related Sexual Violence Through Human Rights Education:
The Case of the Japanese Military's "Comfort Women"

Memorialising Sexual Violence. (n.d.). *Memorials.* **https://gbv-memorials.org.uk/memorials**

Min, P. G. (Ed.). (2025). *Contouring history denialism: The assault on truth about "comfort women."* World Scientific.

Ministry of Culture, Sports and Tourism. (2021). *International Memorial Day for Comfort Women.* **www.korea. net/Events/Overseas/view?articleId=11987**

Ministry of Foreign Affairs of Japan. (n.d.). *Japan's efforts on the issue of comfort women.* **www.mofa.go.jp/policy/ postwar/page22e_000883.html**

Ministry of Foreign Affairs of Japan. (1993, August 4). *Statement by the Chief Cabinet Secretary.* **www.mofa. go.jp/a_o/rp/page25e_000343.html**

Ministry of Foreign Affairs of Japan. (1995, July 1). *Statement by Prime Minister Tomiichi Murayama on the occasion of the establishment of the "Asian Women's Fund."* **www.mofa.go.jp/a_o/rp/page25e_000354.html**

Ministry of Foreign Affairs of Japan. (2015, December 28). *Japan-ROK foreign ministers' meeting.* **www.mofa. go.jp/a_o/na/kr/page4e_000365.html**

Mirindi, J. B. (2024, December 12). *DR Congo: 16 Days of Activism—Working together to end gender-based violence.* World Vision Congo. **www.wvi.org/stories/congo/dr-congo-16-days-activism-working-together-end- gender-based-violence**

Mirkinson, J. (2020). Building the San Francisco memorial: Why the issue of the "comfort women" is still relevant today. In P. G. Min, T. R. Chung, & S. S. Yim (Eds.), *The transnational redress movement for the victims of Japanese military sexual slavery* (pp. 149–177). De Gruyter Oldenbourg.

Moon, K. H. S. (1997). *Sex among allies: Military prostitution in U.S.–Korea relations.* Columbia University Press.

Morris-Suzuki, T. (2015, August 3). You don't want to know about the girls? The "comfort women", the Japanese military and Allied Forces in the Asia–Pacific War. *Asia-Pacific Journal: Japan Focus, 13*(1). **https://apjjf. org/2015/13/31/Tessa-Morris-Suzuki/4352**

Mukwege, D. (2018). *Denis Mukwege: Nobel prize lecture.* The Nobel Prize. **www.nobelprize.org/prizes/ peace/2018/mukwege/lecture**

Mukwege, D. (2021). *The power of women: A doctor's journal of hope and healing.* Flatiron Books.

Mukwege, D. (2025, February 19). Congo is bleeding. Where is the outrage? *The New York Times.* **www.nytimes. com/2025/02/19/opinion/congo-rwanda-rebels-war.html**

Murad, N. (2017). *The last girl: My story of captivity, and my fight against the Islamic State.* Crown.

Murad, N. (2018, December 10). *Nadia Murad: Nobel prize lecture.* The Nobel Prize. **www.nobelprize.org/prizes/ peace/2018/murad/lecture**

Museum of Social Justice. (2024). *"Comfort women" then and now: Who they were and why we should remember them.* **www.museumofsocialjustice.org/comfort-women-then-and-now-who-they-were-and-why-we- should-remember-them.html**

National Council for the Social Studies. (2010). *National curriculum standards for social studies: A framework for teaching, learning, and assessment.*

NBC News. (2007, March 1). *Japan's PM denies "comfort women" coerced.* NBC News. **www.nbcnews.com/id/ wbna10625961**

61

Teaching Conflict-Related Sexual Violence Through Human Rights Education: The Case of the Japanese Military's "Comfort Women"

NBC News. (2014, June 30). *Wounds of war for Japan, Korea re-open with comfort women statue.* **www.nbcnews. com/news/asian-america/wounds-war-japan-korea-re-open-comfort-women-statue-n139481**

Nikkei Asia. (2018, February 16). *Japan's new US envoy eyes removal of "comfort women" statues.* **https://asia. nikkei.com/Politics/International-relations/Japan-s-new-US-envoy-eyes-removal-of-comfort-women-statues**

Nishino, R. (2018). Forcible mobilization: What survivor testimonies tell us. In R. Nishino, P. Kim, & A. Onozawa (Eds.), *Denying the comfort women: The Japanese state's assault on historical truth* (pp. 40–63). Routledge.

Nishino, R., Kim, P., & Onozawa, A. (Eds.). (2018). *Denying the comfort women: The Japanese state's assault on historical truth.* Routledge.

Noh, J. (2023, March 15). German students say university caved to right-wing pressure to remove "comfort women" statue. *Hankyoreh.* **https://english.hani.co.kr/arti/english_edition/e_international/1083751.html**

Norma, C. (2016). *The Japanese comfort women and sexual slavery during the China and Pacific Wars.* Bloomsbury.

N.Y. Sen. Res. 2013-J304 (2013). **www.nysenate.gov/legislation/resolutions/2013/j304**

Oh, B. B. C. (2001). The Japanese imperial system and the Korean "comfort women" of World War II. In M. Stetz & B. B. C. Oh (Eds.), *Legacies of the comfort women of World War II* (pp. 3–25). Routledge.

Olwell, R. (2011). The *Chugakuryoko* and Hogan's heroes: The experience gap between U.S. and Japanese students' knowledge of World War II. *Kappa Delta Pi Record, 47*(3), 129–132.

Onishi, N. (2007, April 25). Japan's "atonement" to former sex slaves stirs anger. *The New York Times.* **www. nytimes.com/2007/04/25/world/asia/25japan.html**

Ornstein, A. C. (2015). Critical issues in teaching. In A. C. Ornstein, E. F. Pajak, & S. B. Ornstein (Eds.), *Contemporary issues in curriculum* (pp. 69–87). Pearson.

Osler, A. (2016). *Human rights and schooling: An ethical framework for teaching for social justice.* Teachers College Press.

Panzi. (n.d.). **https://panzifoundation.org/panzi-hospital/**

Percoco, J., & Richman, M. (1998). *Commemorative sculpture in the United States.* Organization of American Historians; National Center for History in the Schools.

Plucinska, J., Deutsch, A., & Bern, S. (2022, November 23). *Russia accused of using sexual violence as a weapon of war in Ukraine.* CBC. **www.cbc.ca/news/world/russia-ukraine-rape-1.6661735**

Qiu, P. (2013). *Chinese comfort women: Testimonies from imperial Japan's sex slaves.* Oxford University Press.

Ramseyer, J. M. (2021). Contracting for sex in the Pacific War. *International Review of Law and Economics, 65,* Article 105971. **https://doi.org/10.1016/j.irle.2020.105971**

Republic of Rwanda. (2021, April 7). *Rwanda marks the 27th commemoration of the genocide against Tutsi.* **www. gov.rw/blog-detail/rwanda-marks-the-27th-commemoration-of-the-genocide-against-tutsi**

Rittner, C., & Roth, J. K. (Eds.). (2012). *Rape: Weapon of war and genocide.* Paragon House.

Rittner, C., & Roth, J. K. (Eds.). (2016). *Teaching about rape in war and genocide.* Palgrave MacMillan.

62

Teaching Conflict-Related Sexual Violence Through Human Rights Education: The Case of the Japanese Military's "Comfort Women"

Rittner, C., Verdeja, E., von Jeoden-Forgey, E., Slim, H., Baaz, M. E., Stern, M., & Theriault, H. C. (2016). Why teach? In C. Rittner & J. K. Roth (Eds.), *Teaching about rape in war and genocide* (pp. 8–25). Palgrave MacMillan.

Ruff-O'Herne. (2007, February 15). *Hearing on protecting the human rights of "comfort women."* **https://web. archive.org/web/20160303152117/http://archives.republicans.foreignaffairs.house.gov/110/ohe021507. htm**

Ruff-O'Herne, J. (2008). *Fifty years of silence: The extraordinary memoir of a war rape survivor.* Penguin Random House Australia.

Ruiz, E. B. (2020, January 10). Before #MeToo, there were the "comfort women." *The Diplomat.* **https:// thediplomat.com/2020/01/before-metoo-there-were-the-comfort-women**

San Francisco Board of Supervisors Res. 342-15. *Urging the establishment of a memorial for "comfort women."* (2015, September 22). **https://sfbos.org/ftp/uploadedfiles/bdsupvrs/resolutions15/r0342-15.pdf**

San Francisco Board of Supervisors Res. 151-21. *Denouncing the article "Contracting for sex in the Pacific war," by J. Mark Ramseyer of the Japanese Legal Studies at Harvard Law School.* (2021, April 6). **https://sfgov.legistar. com/View.ashx?M=F&ID=9352837&GUID=98ADECEC-34CA-49D8-819C-F0BE187BAE07**

Sander, H. (Director). (1992). *BeFreier und befreite* [Liberators take liberties] [Documentary]. Bremer Institut Film & Fernsehen.

Sarajevo Times. (2023, January 6). *"Women victims of war" association about the Chetnik gathering.* **https:// sarajevotimes.com/women-victims-of-war-association-about-the-chetnik-gathering**

Schellstede, S. C. (Ed.). (2000). *Comfort women speak: Testimony by sex slaves of the Japanese military.* Holmes & Meier.

Schmitt, C. (2013, December 10). *16 Days of Activism: Countering sexual and gender-based violence across the Congo.* UNHCR. **www.unhcr.org/news/stories/16-days-activism-countering-sexual-and-gender-based-violence-across-congo**

Semple, K. (2012, May 19). In New Jersey, memorial for "comfort women deepens old animosity. *The New York Times.* **www.nytimes.com/2012/05/19/nyregion/monument-in-palisades-park-nj-irritates-japanese-officials.html**

Shehu, B. (2024, September 20). *Jahjaga: Wartime sexual violence "an open wound" in Kosovo.* Deutsche Welle. **www.dw.com/en/jahjaga-blame-should-not-be-directed-at-the-survivors-but-at-the-perpetrators-who-used-rape-as-a-weapon-of-war/a-70283271**

Shibata, R. (2013). Globalization, politics of historical memory, and enmification in Sino-Japanese relations. In J. Zajda (Ed.), *Nation-building and history education in a global culture* (pp. 67–81). Springer.

South Sudan Women's Empowerment Network. (n.d.). *Sexual & gender based violence.* **https://sswen.org/policy-politics/**

Stone, K. (2024). Projecting violence elsewhere: Remembering conflict-related sexual violence in Cold War Germany. In C. Bielby & M. P. Davies (Eds.), *Violence elsewhere* [2 volume set] (pp. 18–37). Boydell & Brewer. **https://doi.org/10.2307/jj.15684226.6**

Tanaka, Y. (2002). *Japan's comfort women: Sexual slavery and prostitution during World War II and the U.S. occupation.* Routledge.

63

Teaching Conflict-Related Sexual Violence Through Human Rights Education:
The Case of the Japanese Military's "Comfort Women"

Teo, H. (1996). The continuum of sexual violence in occupied Germany, 1945–49. *Women's History Review, 5*(2), 191–218.

Trial International. (2020, June 19). *Wartime sexual violence survivors: Bosnian and Herzegovina's forgotten ones.* https://trialinternational.org/latest-post/25-years-after-the-war-rights-of-victims-of-sexual-violence-are-still-not-guaranteed-in-bosnia-and-herzegovina/

United Nations. (1948). *Universal declaration of human rights.* www.un.org/en/about-us/universal-declaration-of-human-rights

United Nations. (1995). *Beijing declaration and platform for action.* www.un.org/womenwatch/daw/beijing/pdf/BDPfA E.pdf

United Nations. (1996). *UN Report of the Special Rapporteur.* https://digitallibrary.un.org/record/228137?v=pdf

United Nations. (2000). *Five-year review of the implementation of the Beijing Declaration and Platform for Action (Beijing +5) held in the General Assembly, 5–9 June 2000.* www.un.org/womenwatch/daw/followup/beijing+5.htm

United Nations. (2011). *11. United Nations declaration on human rights education and training (2011).* www.ohchr.org/en/resources/educators/human-rights-education-training/11-united-nations-declaration-human-rights-education-and-training-2011

United Nations. (2025, February 7). *DR Congo: Rights chief warns crisis could worsen, without international action.* https://news.un.org/en/story/2025/02/1159896

United Nations Action Against Sexual Violence in Conflict. (n.d.) www.un.org/sexualviolenceinconflict/about-us/un-action

United Nations Action Against Sexual Violence in Conflict. (2020). *UN action against sexual violence in conflict strategic framework 2020–2025.* https://stoprapenow.org/wordpress/wp-content/uploads/2020/11/10.-UN-Action-Strategic-Framework-2020–2025-endorsed-Aug-2020.pdf

United Nations Economic and Social Council. (1996, January 4). *Report of the Special Rapporteur on violence against women, its causes and consequences, Radhika Coomaraswamy, in accordance with Commission on Human Rights resolution 1994/45.* https://digitallibrary.un.org/record/228137?v=pdf

United Nations Economic and Social Council. (1998, June 22). *Systematic rape, sexual slavery and slavery-like practices during armed conflict: Final report/submitted by Gay J. McDougall, Special Rapporteur.* https://digitallibrary.un.org/record/257682?v=pdf

United Nations Human Rights. (2016, February 16). *committee on the elimination of discrimination against women examines reports of Japan.* www.ohchr.org/en/press-releases/2016/02/committee-elimination-discrimination-against-women-examines-reports-japan

United Nations International Covenant on Civil and Political Rights. (2022, November 30). *Concluding observations on the seventh periodic report of Japan.* https://tbinternet.ohchr.org/_layouts/15/treatybodyexternal/Download.aspx?symbolno=CCPR%2FC%2FJPN%2FCO%2F7&Lang=en

United Nations International Residual Mechanism for Criminal Tribunals. (n.d.). *Kunarac et al. (IT-96–23 & 23/1).* www.icty.org/en/case/kunarac

64

Teaching Conflict-Related Sexual Violence Through Human Rights Education:
The Case of the Japanese Military's "Comfort Women"

United Nations International Residual Mechanism for Criminal Tribunals. (1998, September 2). *News: Historic judgement finds Akayesu guilty of genocide.* **https://unictr.irmct.org/en/news/historic-judgement-finds-akayesu-guilty-genocide**

United Nations Office of the High Commissioner for Human Rights. (2023, November 29). *16 Days of Activism against gender based violence.* **www.ohchr.org/en/women/16-days-activism-against-gender-based-violence**

United Nations Population Fund. (2006, June 21). *First international symposium on sexual violence in conflict and beyond opens today in Brussels.* **www.unfpa.org/press/first-international-symposium-sexual-violence-conflict-and-beyond-opens-today-brussels**

United Nations Secretary-General. (2024). *Conflict-related sexual violence: Report of the United Nations Secretary-General.* **www.un.org/sexualviolenceinconflict/digital-library/reports/sg-reports**

United Nations Security Council. (2008, June 19). *Resolution 1820.* **https://digitallibrary.un.org/record/629882?v=pdf**

United Nations Security Council. (2009, September 30). *Resolution 1888.* **https://digitallibrary.un.org/record/666430?v=pdf**

United Nations Women. (n.d.). *UNITE to end violence against women campaign.* **www.unwomen.org/en/what-we-do/ending-violence-against-women/unite**

U.S. Department of the Treasury. (2018, August 17). *Treasury sanctions commanders and units of the Burmese security forces for serious human rights abuses.* **https://home.treasury.gov/news/press-releases/sm460**

Varona, R. A. (2019, January 5). *Statue of "comfort women" in PH removed after Japanese gov't expresses disappointment.* Asian Journal News. **https://asianjournal.com/philippines/across-the-islands/statue-of-comfort-woman-in-ph-removed-after-japanese-govt-expresses-disappointment/**

Ward, T. J., & Lay, W. D. (2019). *Park statue politics: World War II comfort women memorials in the United States.* E-International Relations.

Westervelt, E. (2009, July 17). *Silence broken on Red Army rapes in Germany.* NPR. **www.npr.org/2009/07/17/106687768/silence-broken-on-red-army-rapes-in-germany**

Williams, J. A. (2025). The future role of the International Assembly: What is its responsibility to contribute to a more humane future? *Journal of International Social Studies, 14*(2), 59–75.

Williams, J. A., & Cha. B. (2023). "Comfort women:" The contention of historical narratives. *Oregon Journal of the Social Studies (special issue), 11*(2), 96–116.

Williams, J. A., & Johnson, M. (2020). Comfort women: Enhancing students' global awareness through human right education. *The Social Studies, 111*(5), 226–233. **https://doi.org/10.1080/00377996.2020.1749016**

Williams, J. A., & Pirlet, C. (2021). Developing global awareness and empathy through the teaching of the Nanjing atrocities. *Oregon Journal of the Social Studies, 9*(2), 12–23.

Women's Active Museum on War and Peace. (n.d.-a). *Map of "comfort stations" of the Japanese military.* **https://wam-peace.org/ianjo**

Women's Active Museum on War and Peace. (n.d.-b). *Resource center.* **https://wam-peace.org/en/ianfu-mondai**

Women's Initiatives for Gender Justice. (n.d.). **https://4genderjustice.org**

65

Teaching Conflict-Related Sexual Violence Through Human Rights Education:
The Case of the Japanese Military's "Comfort Women"

Women's Initiatives for Gender Justice. (2025, February 5). *Crisis in Goma.* **https://4genderjustice.org/our-latest-posts/crisis-in-goma-sexual-violence-and-mass-displacement**

Yamaguchi, T. (2020, March 15). The "history wars" and the "comfort women" issue: Revisionism and the right-wing in contemporary Japan and the U.S. *Asia-Pacific Journal: Japan Focus, 18*(6), Article 5381. **https://apjjf.org/2020/6/yamaguchi**

Yoshimi, Y. (1995). *Comfort women: Sexual slavery in the Japanese military during World War II* (S. O'Brien, Trans.). Columbia University Press.

Yoshimi, Y. (2018). The Kono statement, and the quest for truth. In R. Nishino, P. Kim & A. Onozawa (Eds.), *Denying the comfort women: The Japanese state's assault on historical truth* (pp. 17–39). Routledge.

Yoshimi, Y. (2022, February 8). Response to "Contracting for sex in the Pacific War" by J. Mark Ramseyer (E. Koyama, N. Field, & T. Yamaguchi, Trans.). *International Review of Law and Economics, 76,* Article 106158. **https://doi.org/10.1016/j.irle.2023.106158**

Zhu, L. (2017, March 2). Japan condemned for interference with "comfort women" memorial lawsuit. *China Daily.* **https://europe.chinadaily.com.cn/world/2017–03/02/content_28404481.htm**

66

Teaching Conflict-Related Sexual Violence Through Human Rights Education:
The Case of the Japanese Military's "Comfort Women"

About the Authors

Jing A. Williams, PhD, is Professor of Social Studies Education at the University of South Dakota. In 2024, she was Visiting Professor at Seoul National University of Education. Dr. Williams teaches elementary and secondary social studies methods courses. She served as the president (2018–2020) of the International Assembly of the National Council for the Social Studies (NCSS). Her research focuses on a global perspective in social studies education. She is the lead author of *Teaching with a Global Perspective: Approaches and Strategies for Secondary Social Studies Teachers*, published by NCSS in 2024. She can be reached via email at **Jing.Williams@usd.edu**.

Phyllis Kim is the Executive Director of Comfort Women Action for Redress and Education, a nonprofit, community-based organization in California. She became involved in the "comfort women" movement through the campaign to pass U.S. House Resolution 121 in 2007. Since then, her organization, formerly known as Korean American Forum of California, has led numerous initiatives to raise awareness of the issue in the United States, including establishing the first "girl statue" in Glendale, California, in 2013, collaborating with a multiethnic coalition Comfort Women Justice Coalition to create the San Francisco Comfort Women Memorial and advocating for the inclusion of "comfort women" history in California's 10th-grade World History curriculum. She has also developed educational materials for American high school history teachers, partnered with Sogang University (Seoul, South Korea) to create *Eternal Testimony*, an interactive, conversational video featuring surviving Grandmas (or *Halmoni*, an affectionate term in Korean to refer to Grandmas), and established a "comfort women" online archive at University of California, Los Angeles. She can be reached via email at **ComfortWomenAction@gmail.com**.

67

Teaching Conflict-Related Sexual Violence Through Human Rights Education:
The Case of the Japanese Military's "Comfort Women"

www.ingramcontent.com/pod-product-compliance
Lightning Source LLC
Chambersburg PA
CBHW081200270326
41930CB00014B/3241

*9 7 8 0 8 7 9 8 6 1 4 7 6 *